DATE DUE

DEMCO 38-296

Lemonaid!

A Layperson's Guide to the Automotive Lemon Laws

by

Andrew A. Faglio

Law for the Layperson

Oceana's Legal Almanacs, Second Series

Oceana Publications, Inc.

Dobbs Ferry, NY

Library of Congress Cataloging in Publication Data

Faglio, Andrew A., Lemonaid!: A Layperson's Guide to the Automotive Lemon Laws. 160 pgs.
Includes Appendixes

ISBN: 0-379-11182-9 (paperback)
ISBN: 0-379-11181-0 (cloth)
ISSN: 0075-8582

"Consumer power comes from knowledge and association with other consumers with similar problems. Andrew Faglio has distilled his Lemon experience into a valuable lemonaid guide for other consumers with lemons."

Ralph Nader
Consumer Advocate

ABOUT THE AUTHOR

Presently a resident of New York City, Andrew Faglio is a native born New Yorker who grew up in a middle class, blue collar neighborhood. He holds three college degrees, which include a Masters in Business Administration. As a first-time author, he was able to draw from his work experiences as an aircraft field-engineer and contracts administrator. It was his own personal experience with the Lemon Law that prompted him to write this book.

Acknowledgments

Now that my task is complete, I find myself deeply indebted to a number of people who helped me through my legal battles and the long and arduous task of getting this book published. I must admit, in retrospect, that it was a hell of a lot easier to win the law suit than it was to publish this book!

My personal honor role, denoting each individuals' contribution to my cause, is as follows:

* My Father - advice, encouragement, and the rent free use of his garage for storage of the Fiero for the duration of the lawsuit.

* Maureen Burford - consumer advisor at the New York State Attorney General Office. Maureen was the one who gave me encouragement, guidance and the lead that enabled me to find the right lawyer.

* George Haggerty (and his assistant Janet) - the right lawyer, who presently has a practice in Garden City, N.Y. George and Janet won the case against General Motors for me.

* Robert Abrams - New York State Attorney General. The New York State new and used car lemon laws were put on the books under his administration. He is presently seeing to it that these laws are improved each year so that the consumer is afforded increased protection in the courts.

* Richard Uravitch - a good friend who performed the first edit of my "a little rough around the edges" manuscript.

* Susan De Maio, and Nicholas Brandi - editors extraordinare at Oceana Publications. If you have to work with anyone on your first go around in publishing, Nick and Susan are the two people that you want on your team.

---

on your first go around in publishing, Nick and Susan are the two people that you want on your team.

* Mr. Cohen and Mr. Newman - the decision makers at Oceana Publications who decided to give this unknown author his first shot.

* Richard Fitzgerald - a co-worker who assisted me in overcoming numerous computer hardware glitches.

* Joe Topornycky - numerous "technical assists."

* Chris Cadieux - another co-worker who enabled me to overcome some pretty tough software problems. His computer wizardry enabled me to produce a quality product.

* Anne Ricci - friendship with common roots, and "good conversation".

* Jim Black - a legal eagle who gave unselfishly of his time to assist me in the research and review of this book.

* Joe DiBartolo - my close friend who supplied me with encouragement, the photography in this book, and the lemon that I tied to the Fiero's inside rearview mirror before it was towed away.

THIS BOOK IS LOVINGLY

DEDICATED TO MY

TWO BEST FRIENDS:

ANN AND CARL ...

MY PARENTS

TABLE OF CONTENTS

INTRODUCTION

On August 2, 1984 - I had the most unfortunate experience of purchasing a brand new automobile which, over a short period of time, turned out to be a **LEMON**. For those of you out there that enjoy the pleasures of owning and operating an automobile, this type of experience can cause anger, disappointment, and anxiety. It readily became apparent to me as the weeks and months dragged on that the problems that I was experiencing were not going to be resolved to my satisfaction. I came to the conclusion that the only remedy open to me was to take the manufacturer to task under the provisions of the New York State "Motor Vehicles -- Warranties -- Replacement Requirement" alias "The Lemon Law". I subsequently found a lawyer and pursued the case.

Every step was a learning experience for me. Each step was full of legal hurdles and numerous other obstacles which I learned either to deal with or to circumvent. About halfway through the process I realized that I was on virtually unexplored ground and that I would have to chart a course so that others who followed would know what they were up against and which direction to take.

* HOW THE TEXT IS WRITTEN:

This book is written for those automotive consumers who feel that they are stuck with an automobile manufacturer's **LEMON**; and who are willing to go the distance in order to see to it that the manufacturer is made to bear the financial burden caused by its incompetence. The text is easy to read and supplies the insight, encouragement and guidance required to prepare, fight, and ultimately win a Lemon Law suit. Selected chapters are split into two basic parts. The first part sets forth the letter of the law, while the second part (paralleling the first) tells what my experiences were with regard to my case. As it turned out, this was a case where I was able to recoup the initial purchase price of the vehicle, state sales tax, and my legal fees.

I have since used the methods in this book to guide two of my friends who were having similar problems with their automobiles. One obtained a settlement in small claims court while the other was able to get a 1991 Eldorado replacement vehicle in exchange for his 1989 Coupe deVille plus $4,000.00. The 1989 deVille had 39,000 miles on the odometer at the time that it was returned to the manufacturer. The whole procedure took place within 45 days without the use of a lawyer. There is no arguing with success - LemonAid! worked for me (twice), two of my friends, and it can work for you !

Please keep in mind that I am not advocating that the reader use this book to go out and practice law. It is *not* a legal text written by a lawyer for the legal community. It *is* a book written *by a consumer for other consumers*. This book is a detailed account of what I experienced personally and is to be used as a reference guide. If the reader is unsure of what he or she is doing or is going to have to take the case to court; then by all means refer to the information in Chapter 7 and obtain a lawyer. I am confident that the information in this book will, at a minimum, familiarize you with the law, get you organized, build your case, and take you through the entire arbitration procedure without the use of a lawyer. For most consumers, this will be enough to win and to obtain a refund.

* WHO THIS BOOK IS FOR:

I feel obliged to state one thing from the start, one which requires the reader to undergo a little self-analysis. The course one has to take to fight and ultimately defeat an automobile manufacturer requires some time and effort. As such you should ask yourself the following questions:

*** Are you the type of person who backs down even when you know you are right?**

*** Are you inclined to grow impatient and "throw in the towel" when you suffer a few minor set backs or when things do not move as fast as you would like them to?**

*** Are you the type of person who places time and money ahead of your principles?**

* Are you the type of person who is convinced that "You can't fight city hall" ?

(And WIN !!!)

If the answer to any or all of the above questions is yes... better put this book back on the shelf and go read a nice novel!

CHAPTER 1

THE NEW VEHICLE LEMON LAW

The first step in any legal procedure is to obtain a working knowledge of the law as it appears in its most current version. This chapter will accomplish the following:

(I) Reprint the New York New Vehicle Lemon Law in its most current version.

(II) Select, explain, and summarize the key points of the law.

(III) Illustrate how my case involving a new 1984 Pontiac Fiero SE satisfied the provisions of the law.

The reader should note that Lemon Laws are written and enforced on the state level and will vary in breadth and scope according to the state in which the lawsuit is initiated. Some states, at present, do not have any Lemon Laws in effect; while other states, like New York, have laws which cover both new and used vehicles. The New York State *Used Vehicle* Lemon Law is listed and outlined in Chapter 2 of this book. I suggest that any reader, who has purchased and registered a new or used vehicle outside of New York State, first consult the 50 state new/used lemon law matrix that is located in Appendix D in the back of this book and then contact their local state attorney general's office, county or public/college library in order to obtain a copy of the law. Copies of the law for New York State can be found in the **McKinney's Consolidated Laws of New York Annotated.** The reader should review the law and understand it so that he or she will be able to chart a course of action in addition to having the ability to speak intelligently during the arbitration proceedings or with their lawyer should they have to go the full distance and bring the case to court.

I purchased my Pontiac Fiero SE in New York State on August 2,1984. As such, it fell under the 1983 New York State Session Laws-Chapter 444. The law is entitled "Motor Vehicles - Warranties -

Replacement Requirement.'' The law, for *new* vehicles purchased in New York State as it presently appears on the books is reproduced in its entirety below.

* THE LAW AS IT APPEARS ON THE BOOKS: -- NEW YORK STATE NEW CAR LEMON LAW --

General Business Law: 198-a. Warranties

(a) As used in this section:

(1) ''Consumer'' means the purchaser, lessee or transferee, other than for purposes of resale, of a motor vehicle which is used primarily for personal, family or household purposes and any other person entitled by the terms of the manufacturer's warranty to enforce the obligations of such warranty;

(2) ''Motor vehicle'' means a motor vehicle excluding motorcycles and off road vehicles, which was subject to a manufacturer's express warranty at the time of original delivery and either (i) was purchased, leased or transferred in this state within either the first eighteen thousand miles of operation or two years from the date of original delivery, whichever is earlier, or (ii) is registered in this state;

(3) ''Manufacturer's express warranty'' or ''warranty'' means the written warranty, so labeled, of the manufacturer of a new motor vehicle, including any terms or conditions precedent to the enforcement of obligations under that warranty.

(4) ''Mileage deduction formula'' means the mileage which is in excess of twelve thousand miles times the purchase price, or the lease price if applicable, of the vehicle divided by one hundred thousand miles.

(5) ''Lessee'' means any consumer who leases a motor vehicle pursuant to a written lease agreement which provides that the lessee is responsible for repairs to such motor vehicle.

(6) ''Lease price'' means the aggregate of:

(i) the lessor's actual purchase cost;

(ii) the freight cost, if applicable;

(iii) the cost for accessories, if applicable;

(iv) any fee paid to another to obtain the lease; and

(v) an amount equal to five percent of the lessor's actual purchase cost as prescribed in subparagraph (i) of this paragraph.

(7) "Service fees" means the portion of a lease payment attributable to:

(i) an amount for earned interest calculated on the rental payments previously paid to the lessor for the leased vehicle at an annual rate equal to two points above the prime rate in effect on the date of the execution of the lease; and

(ii) any insurance or other costs expended by the lessor for the benefit of the lessee.

(8) "Capitalized cost" means the aggregate deposit and rental payments previously paid to the lessor for the leased vehicle less service fees.

(b) (1) If a new motor vehicle which is sold and registered in this state does not conform to all express warranties during the first eighteen thousand miles of operation or during the period of two years following the date of original delivery of the motor vehicle to such consumer, whichever is the earlier date, the consumer shall during such period report the nonconformity, defect or condition to the manufacturer, its agent or its authorized dealer. If the notification is received by the manufacturer's agent or authorized dealer, the agent or dealer shall within seven days forward written notice thereof to the manufacturer by certified mail, return receipt requested, and shall include in such notice a statement indicating whether or not such repairs have been undertaken. The manufacturer, its agent or its authorized dealer shall correct said nonconformity, defect or condition at no charge to the consumer, notwithstanding the fact that such repairs are made after the expiration of such period of operation or such two year period.

(b) (2) If a manufacturer's agent or authorized dealer refuses to undertake repairs within seven days of receipt of the notice by a consumer of a nonconformity, defect or condition pursuant to paragraph one of this subdivision, the consumer may immediately forward written notice of such refusal to the manufacturer by certified mail, return receipt requested. The manufacturer or its agent shall have twenty days from receipt of such notice of refusal to commence such repairs. If within such twenty day period, the manufacturer or its authorized agent fails to commence such repairs, the manufacturer at the option of the consumer, shall replace the motor vehicle with a comparable motor vehicle, or accept return of the vehicle from the consumer and refund to the consumer the full purchase price or, if applicable,the lease price and any trade-in allowance plus fees and charges. Such fees and charges shall include but not be limited to all license fees, registration fees and any similar governmental charges, less an allowance for the consumer's use of the vehicle in excess of the first twelve thousand miles of operation pursuant to the mileage deduction formula defined in paragraph four of subdivision (a) of this section, and a reasonable allowance for any damage not attributable to normal wear or improvements.

(c) (1) If, within the period specified in subdivision (b) of this section, the manufacturer or its agents or authorized dealers are unable to repair or correct any defect or condition which substantially impairs the value of the motor vehicle to the consumer after a reasonable number of attempts, the manufacturer, at the option of the consumer, shall replace the motor vehicle with a comparable motor vehicle, or accept return of the vehicle from the consumer and refund to the consumer the full purchase price or,if applicable, the lease price and any trade-in allowance plus fees and charges. Any return of a motor vehicle may, at the option of the consumer, be made to the dealer or other authorized agent of the manufacurer who sold such vehicle to the consumer or to the dealer or other authorized agent who attempted to repair or correct the defect or condition which necessitated the return and shall not be subject to any further shipping charges. Such fees and charges shall include but not be limited to all license fees, registration fees and any similar governmental charges, less an allowance for the consumer's use of the vehicle in excess of the first twelve thousand miles of operation pursuant to the mileage deduction formula defined in paragraph four of subdivision (a) of this section, and a reasonable allowance for any damage not attributable to normal wear or improvements.

(2) A manufacturer which accepts return of the motor vehicle because the motor vehicle does not conform to its warranty shall notify the commissioner of the department of motor vehicles that the motor vehicle was returned to the manufacturer for nonconformity to its warranty and shall disclose, in accordance with the provisions of section four hundred seventeen-a of the vehicle and traffic law prior to resale either at wholesale or retail, that it was previously returned to the manufacturer for nonconformity to its warranty. Refunds shall be made to the consumer and lien holder, if any, as their interests may appear on the records of ownership kept by the department of motor vehicles. Refunds shall be accompanied by the proper application for creditor refund of state and local sales taxes as published by the department of taxation and finance and by a notice that the sales tax paid on the purchase price, lease price or portion thereof being refunded is refundable by the Commissioner of Taxation and Finance in accordance with the provisions of subdivision (f) of section eleven hundred thirty-nine of the tax law. If applicable, refunds shall be made to the lessor and lessee as their interests may appear on the records of ownership kept by the department of motor vehicles, as follows: the lessee shall receive the capitalized cost and the lessor shall receive the lease price less the aggregate deposit and rental payments previously paid to the lessor for the leased vehicle. The terms of the lease shall be deemed terminated contemporaneously with the date of the arbitrator's decision and award and no penalty for early termination shall be assessed as a result thereof. Refunds shall be accompanied by the proper application form for credit or refund of state and local sales tax as published by the department of taxation and finance and a notice that the sales tax paid on the lease price or portion thereof being refunded is refundable by the Commissioner of Taxation and Finance in accordance with the provisions of subdivision (f) of section eleven hundred thirty-nine of the tax law.

(3) It shall be an affirmative defense to any claim under this section that:

(i) the nonconformity, defect or condition does not substantially impair such value; or

(ii) the nonconformity, defect or condition is the result of abuse, neglect or unauthorized modifications or alterations of the motor vehicle.

(d) It shall be presumed that a reasonable number of attempts have been undertaken to conform a motor vehicle to the applicable express warranties, if:

(1) the same nonconformity, defect or condition has been subject to repair four or more times by the manufacturer or its agents or authorized dealers within the first eighteen thousand miles of operation or during the period of two years following the date of original delivery of the motor vehicle to a consumer, whichever is the earlier date, but such nonconformity, defect or condition continues to exist; or

(2) the vehicle is out of service by reason of repair of one or more nonconformities, defects or conditions for a cumulative total of thirty or more calendar days during either period, whichever is the earlier date.

(e) The term of an express warranty, the two year warranty period and the thirty day out of service period shall be extended by any time during which repair services are not available to the consumer because of a war, invasion or strike, fire, flood or other natural disaster.

(f) Nothing in this section shall in any way limit the rights or remedies which are otherwise available to a consumer under any other law.

(g) If a manufacturer has established an informal dispute settlement mechanism, such mechanism shall comply in all respects with the provisions of this section and the provisions of subdivision (c) of this section concerning refunds or replacement shall not apply to any consumer who has not first resorted to such mechanism. In the event that an arbitrator in such an informal dispute mechanism awards a refund or replacement vehicle, he or she shall not reduce the award to an amount less than the full purchase price or the lease price, if applicable, or a vehicle of equal value, plus all fees and charges except to the extent such reductions are specifically permitted under subdivision (c) of this section.

(h) A manufacturer shall have up to thirty days from the date the consumer notifies the manufacturer of his or her acceptance of the arbitrator's decision to comply with the terms of that decision. Failure to comply with the thirty day limitation shall also entitle the consumer to recover a fee of twenty-five dollars for each business day of noncompliance up to five hundred dollars. Provided, however, that nothing contained in this subdivision shall impose any liability on a manufacturer where a delay beyond the thirty day period is attributable to a consumer who has requested a replacement vehicle built to order or with options that are not comparable to the vehicle being replaced or otherwise made compliance impossible within said period. In no event shall a consumer who has resorted to an informal dispute settlement mechanism be precluded from seeking the rights or remedies available by law.

(i) Any agreement entered into by a consumer for the purchase of a new motor vehicle which waives, limits or disclaims the rights set forth in this section shall be void as contrary to public policy. Said rights shall inure to a subsequent transferee of such motor vehicle.

(j) Any action brought pursuant to this section shall be commenced within four years of the date of original delivery of the motor vehicle to the consumer.

(k) Each consumer shall have the option of submitting any dispute arising under this section upon the payment of a prescribed filing fee to an alternate arbitration mechanism established pursuant to regulations promulgated hereunder by the New York state attorney general. Upon application of the consumer and payment of the filing fee, all manufacturers shall submit to such alternate arbitration.

Such alternate arbitration shall be conducted by a professional arbitrator or arbitration firm appointed by and under regulations established by the New York State Attorney General. Such mechanism shall insure the personal objectivity of its arbitrators and the right of each party to present its case, to be in attendance during any presentation made by the other party and to rebut or refute such presentation. In all other respects, such alternate arbitration mechanism shall be governed by article seventy-five of the civil practice law and rules.

(1) A court may award reasonable attorney's fees to a prevailing plaintiff or to a consumer who prevails in any judicial action or proceeding arising out of an arbitration proceeding held pursuant to subdivision (k) of this section. In the event a prevailing plaintiff is required to retain the services of an attorney to enforce the collection of an award granted pursuant to this section, the court may assess against the manufacturer reasonable attorney's fees for services rendered to enforce collection of said amount.

(m)(1) Each manufacturer shall require that each informal dispute settlement mechanism used by it provide, at a minimum, the following:

(i) that the arbitrators participating in such mechanism are trained in arbitration and familiar with the provisions of this section, that the arbitrators and consumers who request arbitration are provided with a written copy of the provisions of this section, together with the notice set forth below entitled "NEW CAR LEMON LAW BILL OF RIGHTS," and that consumers, upon request, are given an opportunity to make an oral presentation to the arbitrator;

(ii) that the rights and procedures used in the mechanism comply with federal regulations promulgated by the federal trade commission relating to informal dispute settlement mechanisms; and

(iii) that the remedies set forth under subdivision (c) of this section are awarded if, after a reasonable number of attempts have been undertaken under subdivision (d) of this section to conform the vehicle to the express warranties, the defect or nonconformity still exists.

(2) The following notice shall be provided to consumers and arbitrators and shall be printed in conspicuous ten point bold face type:

NEW CAR LEMON LAW BILL OF RIGHTS

(1) IN ADDITION TO ANY WARRANTIES OFFERED BY THE MANUFACTURER, YOUR NEW CAR, IF PURCHASED AND REGISTERED IN NEW YORK STATE, IS WARRANTED AGAINST ALL MATERIAL DEFECTS FOR EIGHTEEN THOUSAND MILES OR TWO YEARS, WHICHEVER COMES FIRST.

(2) YOU MUST REPORT ANY PROBLEMS TO THE MANUFACTURER, ITS AGENT, OR AUTHORIZED DEALER.

(3) UPON NOTIFICATION, THE PROBLEM MUST BE CORRECTED FREE OF CHARGE.

(4) IF THE SAME PROBLEM CANNOT BE REPAIRED AFTER FOUR OR MORE ATTEMPTS, OR IF YOUR CAR IS OUT OF SERVICE TO REPAIR A PROBLEM FOR A TOTAL OF THIRTY DAYS DURING THE WARRANTY PERIOD; OR IF THE MANUFACTURER OR ITS AGENT REFUSES TO REPAIR A SUBSTANTIAL DEFECT OR CONDITION WITHIN TWENTY DAYS OF RECEIPT OF NOTICE SENT BY YOU TO THE MANUFACTURER BY CERTIFIED MAIL, RETURN RECEIPT REQUESTED; THEN YOU MAY BE ENTITLED TO EITHER A COMPARABLE CAR OR A REFUND OR YOUR PURCHASE PRICE, PLUS LICENSE AND REGISTRATION FEES, MINUS A MILEAGE ALLOWANCE ONLY IF THE VEHICLE HAS BEEN DRIVEN MORE THAN 12,000 MILES. SPECIAL NOTIFICATION REQUIREMENTS MAY APPLY TO MOTOR HOMES.

(5) A MANUFACTURER MAY DENY LIABILITY IF THE PROBLEM IS CAUSED BY ABUSE, NEGLECT, OR UNAUTHORIZED MODIFICATION OF THE CAR.

(6) A MANUFACTURER MAY REFUSE TO EXCHANGE A COMPARABLE CAR OR REFUND YOUR PURCHASE PRICE IF THE PROBLEM DOES NOT SUBSTANTIALLY IMPAIR THE VALUE OF YOUR CAR.

(7) IF A MANUFACTURER HAS ESTABLISHED AN ARBITRATION PROCEDURE, THE MANUFACTURER MAY REFUSE TO EXCHANGE A COMPARABLE CAR OR REFUND YOUR PURCHASE PRICE UNTIL YOU FIRST RESORT TO THE PROCEDURE.

(8) IF THE MANUFACTURER DOES NOT HAVE AN ARBITRATION PROCEDURE, YOU MAY RESORT TO ANY REMEDY BY LAW AND MAY BE ENTITLED TO YOUR ATTORNEY'S FEES IF YOU PREVAIL.

(9) NO CONTRACT OR AGREEMENT CAN VOID ANY OF THESE RIGHTS.

(10) AS AN ALTERNATIVE TO THE ARBITRATION PROCEDURE MADE AVAILABLE THROUGH THE MANUFACTURER, YOU MAY INSTEAD CHOOSE TO SUBMIT YOUR CLAIM TO AN INDEPENDENT ARBITRATOR, APPROVED BY THE ATTORNEY GENERAL. YOU MAY HAVE TO PAY A FEE FOR SUCH AN ARBITRATION. CONTACT YOUR LOCAL CONSUMER OFFICE OR ATTORNEY GENERAL'S OFFICE TO FIND OUT HOW TO ARRANGE FOR INDEPENDENT ARBITRATION.

(3) All informal dispute settlement mechanisms shall maintain the following records:

(i) the number of purchase price and lease price refunds and vehicle replacements requested, the number of each awarded in arbitration, the amount of each award and the number of awards that were compiled with in a timely manner;

(ii) the number of awards where additional repairs or a warranty extension was the most prominent remedy, the amount or value of each award, and the number of such awards that were complied with in a timely manner;

(iii) the number and total dollar amount of awards where some form of reimbursement for expenses or compensation for losses was the most prominent remedy, the amount or value of each award and the number of such awards that were complied with in a timely manner; and

(iv) the average number of days from the date of a consumer's initial request to arbitrate until the date of the final arbitrator's decision and the average number of days from the date of the final arbitrator's decision to the date on which performance was satisfactorily carried out.

(n) Special provisions applicable to motor homes:

(1) To the extent that the provisions of this subdivision are inconsistent with the other provisions of this section, the provisions of this subdivision shall apply.

(2) For purposes of this section, the manufacturer of a motor home is any person, partnership, corporation, factory branch, or other entity engaged in the business of manufacturing or assembling new motor homes for sale in this state.

(3) This section does not apply to nonconformities, defects or conditions in motor home systems, fixtures, components, appliances, furnishings or accessories that are residential in character.

(4) If, within the period specified in subdivision (b) of this section, the manufacturer of a motor home or its agents or its

authorized dealers or repair shops to which they refer a customer are unable to repair or correct any defect or condition which substantially impairs the value of the motor home to the consumer after a reasonable number of attempts, the motor home manufacturer, at the option of the consumer, shall replace the motor home with a comparable motor home, or accept return of the motor home from the consumer and refund to the consumer the full purchase price or, if applicable, the lease price and any trade-in allowance plus fees and charges as well as the other fees and charges set forth in paragraph one of subdivision (c) of this section.

(5) If an agent or authorized dealer of a motor home manufacturer or a repair shop to which they refer a consumer refuses to undertake repairs within seven days of receipt of notice by a consumer of a nonconformity, defect or condition pursuant to paragraph one of subdivision (b) of this section, the consumer may immediately forward written notice of such refusal to the motor home manufacturer by certified mail, return receipt requested. The motor home manufacturer or its authorized agent or a repair shop to which they refer a consumer shall have twenty days from receipt of such notice of refusal to commence such repairs. If within such twenty-day period, the motor home manufacturer or its authorized agent or repair shop to which they refer a consumer, fails to commence such repairs, the motor home manufacturer, at the option of the consumer, shall replace the motor home with a comparable motor home, or accept return of the motor home from the consumer and refund to the consumer the full purchase price or, if applicable, the lease price, and any trade-in allowance or other charges or allowances as set forth in paragraph two of subdivision (b) of this section.

(6) If within the period specified in subdivision (b) of this section, the same nonconformity, defect or condition in a motor home has been subject to repair three times or a motor home has been out of service by reason of repair for twenty-one days, whichever occurs first, the consumer must have reported

this to the motor home manufacturer or its authorized dealer by certified mail, return receipt requested, prior to instituting any proceeding or other action pursuant to this section provided, however, that the special notification requirements of this paragraph shall only apply if the manufacturer or its authorized dealer provides a prior written copy of the requirements of this paragraph to the consumer and receipt of the notice is acknowledged by the consumer in writing. If the consumer who has received notice from the manufacturer fails to comply with the special notification requirements of this paragraph, additional repair attempts or days out of service by reason of repair shall not be taken into account in determining whether the consumer is entitled to a remedy provided in paragraph four of this subdivision. However, additional repair attempts or days out of service by reason of repair that occur after the consumer complies with such special notification requirements shall be taken into account in making that determination.

(7) Nothing in this section shall in any way limit any rights, remedies or causes of action that a consumer or motor home manufacturer may otherwise have against the manufacturer of the motor home's chassis, or its propulsion and other components.

WHAT IT MEANS IN SIMPLE ENGLISH:

What all this means in layman's terms is:

1.) All new car warranties for motor vehicles purchased new in the State of New York on or after September 1, 1983 are automatically extended to a period of 2 years or 18,000 miles - whichever occurs first.

2.) In the aforementioned period (Section 1), the owner must have returned the vehicle to the manufacturer or dealer for four or more unsuccessful repair attempts of the same defect which substantially impacts the value or safety of the vehicle.

3.) The vehicle is out of service for repairs, for the period called out in section one, for a cumulative total of 30 or more calendar days.

4.) The law covers only those leased cars where the lessee is responsible for repairs of the car. The legality of having vehicles that are owned by a business covered by this law is presently being decided in the courts.

5.) The consumer has up to 4 years after purchase/delivery to initiate the lawsuit.

The law views any vehicle which meets the above requirements as a "Lemon" and therefore entitles you, the consumer, to a full refund of the purchase price of the vehicle (including all sales tax, license and registration fees) plus - and this is a very important plus - full recovery of all court and attorney's fees.

A deduction of the refund can be made by the courts for any mileage on the vehicle in excess of 12,000 miles. This basically comes out to 1/100th of the total purchase price of the vehicle for every thousand miles over 12,000 on the odometer as called out in the New York State law. The consumer also has the choice of opting for a comparable vehicle from the manufacturer as a replacement.

I chose to seek the full refund by following the logic - why should I allow the manufacturer to replace a vehicle at their cost with one for which I paid retail. The grief they had caused me at this point convinced me that I wanted to recover as much from them as the law would allow.

*NEW/PENDING AMENDMENTS

I have added this list which explains the new and pending amendments to the New York State New Vehicle Lemon Law in an effort to keep this writing as current as possible at the time of its publication. It outlines recent developments in the law that could prove to be of great

THE NEW VEHICLE LEMON LAW

value for the consumers in New York State. This list represents amendments to the law that have recently been incorporated into the law or are waiting for final approval by the state legislature. They are as follows:

The law has been updated to define a new motor vehicle as any vehicle that has less than 18,000 miles on the odometer or is less than two years old. This covers any vehicle which is purchased, leased, or transferred to other owners within the aforementioned period. Vehicle mileage and age now becomes the sole determinant of the vehicle status under the law. The gray area between the New York State **New** and New York State **Used** Vehicle Lemon Law should be effectively eliminated by this change. This is good news for those people who have purchased or leased a "demonstrator" vehicle.

Another benefit of the updated law is its coverage of all vehicles that are either purchased *or* registered in New York State. This protects consumers who live on state borders - giving them the option to purchase a vehicle over the line and register it in their home state or conversely purchase it in their home state and register it in another. Military personnel will be particularly pleased with this latest addition.

Consumers of motorhomes are now covered by a specific amendment which states that it is the motorhome manufacturer who has the prime responsibility to comply with the statutes of the lemon law. He/She or his/her authorized dealer will be the single point of contact for all vehicle repairs and all lemon law actions. It will however state that the motorhome manufacturer will be able to seek relief from the manufacturer of the chassis and propulsion components in cases where losses occur due to lemon law actions. The law only applies to the motor home chassis and propulsion components - the ones that it has in common with all other motor vehicles.

Also, according to the law in its newly amended form, the consumer will not be subject to any further shipping charges associated with the return of a vehicle to the manufacturer. This improvement prevents manufacturers from insisting that the vehicle in question be returned to a zone office instead of a local dealership prior to receipt of refund or replacement vehicle. The New York State Attorney General observed that some consumers had to take off from work and drive or have the vehicle transported over 100 miles.

Legal fees incurred by the consumer in an effort to get the manufacturer or dealer to comply with the arbitrator or court ruling are now covered by the law.

It should be noted that a recent ruling has made it illegal for the manufacturer or authorized dealer to charge the consumer for any warranty work (including any "deductable") for any warranty work performed during the period that the vehicle is covered by the Lemon Law. You may be entitled to a refund. For more information contact The Attorney General Office or write to:

Deductable Refunds

Attorney General Robert Abrams

Lemon Law Repairs

Consumer Frauds Bureau

120 Broadway

New York, N.Y. 10271

Lastly, tougher and easier to follow procedures are being instituted to insure that any vehicle judged to be a lemon comes with a title "branding" it as such.

* MY EXPERIENCE WITH THE FIERO:

As was stated previously, my case involved the purchase of a new 1984 Pontiac Fiero SE on August 2, 1984 from a local dealership. I was forced to return the vehicle to the dealership 7 times for the same complaint (9 times total) within a 12,000 mile / 11 mouth period. These trips to the dealer resulted in the loss of the vehicle for a total of 43 days!

THE NEW VEHICLE LEMON LAW

The law requires either 4 unsuccessful repair attempts for the same defect or loss of the vehicle for a total of 30 days within the prescribed 2 year / 18,000 mile period. Either condition would have been sufficient - my case involved both. A more detailed description of the vehicle defects that I had to contend with are in Chapter 3.

To add insult to injury, I was told that after my **9 visits** to the dealership and loss of the vehicle for **43 days** I would have to return the Fiero to the dealership for a tenth time so that they could replace the engine block due to an internal crack in the water cooling jackets. They estimated that it would take around 7 days to effect the repair. I asked them for a completely new engine. When they refused, I took them to court.

Keep in mind that my case invoked the 1985 version of the New York State new motor vehicle lemon law. The law, as it appears in the beginning of this chapter is the latest 1991 version. It took me eighteen months and the use of a lawyer to obtain my winning judgement under the 1985 version of the law. My recent application of the 1991 version of the law for a co-worker took less than 45 days. We were able to obtain a winning judgement from the manufacturer, without the use of a lawyer, the day before the arbitration hearing was scheduled to take place.

What I am stressing here is that the original legal definition of what a "lemon" is, the nucleus of the law, has remained the same from the original 1983 version up through the present 1991 version. All revisions to the original 1983 version of the law have served only to enhance the *breath* and scope of the law as it relates to which consumers and what type of vehicles are covered. These revisions have also established a system that yields a more expedient and just method of obtaining a judgement for the consumer. The law just keeps getting better!

The reader should know that an arbitration procedure is required in New York State before they can take the case to court. So, if you meet the requirements and have the will to fight it out...READ ON!

CHAPTER 2

THE USED VEHICLE LEMON LAW

The first step in any legal procedure is to obtain a working knowledge of the law as it appears in its most current version. This chapter will accomplish the following:

I) Reprint the New York State Used Vehicle Lemon Law in its most current version

II) Select, explain, and summarize the key points of the law.

The reader should note that Lemon Laws are written and enforced on the state level and will vary in breadth and scope according to the state in which the lawsuit is initiated. Some states, at present, do not have any Lemon Laws in effect; while other states, like New York, have laws which cover both new and used vehicles. The New York State new vehicle lemon law is reprinted and commented on in Chapter 1 of this book. I suggest that any reader, who has purchased and registered a used vehicle outside of New York State, first consult the 50 state new/used lemon law matrix located in Appendix D in the back of this book and then contact their local state attorney general's office, county or public/college library in order to obtain a copy of the law. Copies of the law, for New York State, can be found in the **McKinney's Consolidated Laws of New York Annotated**. The reader should review the law and understand it so that he or she will be able to chart a course of action in addition to being able to speak intelligently during the arbitration proceedings or with their lawyer should they have to go the full distance and try the case in court.

The law for **used** vehicles purchased in New York State as it presently appears on the books is reproduced in its entirety below.

LEMONAID!

General Business Law: Section 198-b.

Sale or Lease of Used Motor Vehicles

a. Definitions. As used in this section, the following words shall have the following meanings:

1. "Consumer" means the purchaser or lessee, other than for purposes of resale, of a used motor vehicle primarily used for personal, family, or household purposes and subject to a warranty, and the spouse or child of the purchaser or the lessee if either such motor vehicle or the lease of such motor vehicle is transferred to the spouse or child during the duration of any warranty applicable to such motor vehicle, and any other person entitled by the terms of such warranty to enforce the obligations of the warranty;

2. "Used motor vehicle" means a motor vehicle, excluding motorcycles, motor homes and off-road vehicles, which has been purchased, leased, or transferred either after eighteen thousand miles of operation or two years from the date of original delivery, whichever is earlier;

3. "Dealer" means any person or business which sells, offers for sale, leases or offers for lease a used vehicle after selling, offering for sale, leasing or offering for lease three or more used vehicles in the previous twelve month period, but does not include:

(a) a bank or financial institution except in the case of a lease of a used motor vehicle,

(b) a business selling a used vehicle to an employee of that business,

(c) a regulated public utility which sells at public auction vehicles used in the ordinary course of its operations, provided that any advertisements of such sales conspicuously disclose the "as is" nature of the sale,

(d) a lessor selling a leased vehicle to that vehicle's lessee, a family member of the lessee, or an employee of the lessee,

(e) or the state, its agencies, bureaus, boards, commissions and authorities, and all of the political subdivisions of the state, including the agencies and authorities of such subdivisions;

4. "Warranty" means any undertaking in connection with the sale or lease by a dealer of a used motor vehicle to refund, repair, replace, maintain or take other action with respect to such used motor vehicle and provided at no extra charge beyond the price of the used motor vehicle;

5. "Service contract" means a contract in writing for any period of time or any specific mileage to refund, repair, replace, maintain or take other action with respect to a used motor vehicle and provided at an extra charge beyond the price of the used motor vehicle or of the lease contract for the used motor vehicle;

6. "Repair insurance" means a contract in writing for any period of time or any specific mileage to refund, repair, replace, maintain or take other action with respect to a used motor vehicle and which is regulated by the insurance department.

b. Written warranty required; terms.

1. No dealer shall sell or lease a used motor vehicle to a consumer without giving the consumer a written warranty which shall at minimum apply for the following terms:

(a) If the used motor vehicle has thirty-six thousand miles or less, the warranty shall be at minimum ninety days or four thousand miles, whichever comes first.

LEMONAID!

(b) If the used motor vehicle has more than thirty-six thousand miles, but less than eighty thousand miles, the warranty shall be at minimum sixty days or three thousand miles, whichever comes first.

(c) If the used motor vehicle has eighty thousand miles or more but no more than one hundred thousand miles, the warranty shall be at a minimum thirty days or one thousand miles, whichever comes first.

2. The written warranty shall require the dealer or his agent to repair or, at the election of the dealer, reimburse the consumer for the reasonable cost of repairing the failure of a covered part. Covered parts shall at least include the following items:

(a) Engine. All lubricated parts, water pump, fuel pump, manifolds, engine block, cylinder head, rotary engine housings and flywheel.

(b) Transmission. The transmission case, internal parts, and the torque converter.

(c) Drive axle. Front and rear drive axle housings and internal parts, axle shafts, propeller shafts and universal joints.

(d) Brakes. Master cylinder, vacuum assist booster, wheel cylinders, hydraulic lines and fittings and disc brake calipers.

(e) Radiator.

(f) Steering. The steering gear housing and all internal parts, power steering pump, valve body, piston and rack.

(g) Alternator, generator, starter, ignition system excluding the battery.

3. Such repair or reimbursement shall be made by the dealer notwithstanding the fact that the warranty period has expired, provided the consumer notifies the dealer of the failure of a covered part within the specified warranty period.

4. The written warranty may contain additional language excluding coverage:

(a) for a failure of a covered part caused by a lack of customary maintenance;

(b) for a failure of a covered part caused by collision, abuse, negligence, theft, vandalism, fire or other casualty and damage from the environment (windstorm, lightning, road hazards, etc.);

(c) if the odometer has been stopped or altered such that the vehicle's actual mileage cannot be readily determined or if any covered part has been altered such that a covered part was thereby caused to fail;

(d) for maintenance services and the parts used in connection with such services such as seals, gaskets, oil or grease unless required in connection with the repair of a covered part;

(e) for a motor tuneup;

(f) for a failure resulting from racing or other competition;

(g) for a failure caused by towing a trailer or another vehicle unless the used motor vehicle is equipped for this as recommended by the manufacturer;

(h) if the used motor vehicle is used to carry passengers for hire;

(i) if the used motor vehicle is rented to someone other than the consumer as defined in paragraph one of subdivision a of this section;

(j) for repair of valves and/or rings to correct low compression and/or oil consumption which are considered normal wear;

(k) to the extent otherwise permitted by law, for property damage arising or allegedly arising out of failure of a covered part; and

LEMONAID!

(l) to the extent otherwise permitted by law, for loss of the use of the used motor vehicle, loss of time, inconvenience, commercial loss or consequential damages.

c. Failure to honor warranty.

1. If the dealer or his agent fails to correct a malfunction or defect as required by the warranty specified in this section which substantially impairs the value of the used motor vehicle to the consumer after a reasonable period of time, the dealer shall accept return of the used motor vehicle from the consumer and refund to the consumer the full purchase price or in the case of a lease contract all payments made under the contract, including sales or compensating use tax, less a reasonable allowance for any damage not attributable to normal wear or usage, and adjustment for any modifications which either increase or decrease the market value of the vehicle or of the lease contract, and in the case of a lease contract, shall cancel all further payments due from the consumer under the lease contract. In determining the purchase price to be refunded or in determining all payments made under a lease contract to be refunded, the purchase price, or all payments made under a lease contract, shall be deemed equal to the sum of the actual cash difference paid for the used motor vehicle, or for the lease contract, plus, if the dealer elects to not return any vehicles traded-in by the consumer, the wholesale value of any such traded-in vehicles as listed in the National Auto Dealers Association Used Car Guide, or such other guide as may be specified in regulations promulgated by the commissioner of motor vehicles, as adjusted for mileage, improvements, and any major physical or mechanical defects in the traded-in vehicle at the time of the trade-in. The dealer selling or leasing the used motor vehicle shall deliver to the consumer a written notice including conspicuous language indicating that if the consumer should be entitled to a refund pursuant to this section, the value of any vehicle traded-in by the consumer, if the dealer elects to not return it to the consumer, for purposes of determining the amount of such refund will be determined by reference to the National Auto Dealers Association Used Car Guide wholesale value, or such other guide as may be approved by the commissioner of motor vehicles, as adjusted for mileage, improvements, and any major physical or mechanical defects, rather than the value listed in the sales contract.

THE USED VEHICLE LEMON LAW

Refunds shall be made to the consumer and lien holder, if any, as their interests may appear on the records of ownership kept by the department of motor vehicles. If the amount to be refunded to the lien holder will be insufficient to discharge the lien, the dealer shall notify the consumer in writing by registered or certified mail that the consumer has thirty days to pay the lien holder the amount which, together with the amount to be refunded by the dealer, will be sufficient to discharge the lien. The notice to the consumer shall contain conspicuous language warning the consumer that failure to pay such funds to the lien holder within thirty days will terminate the dealer's obligation to provide a refund. If the consumer fails to make such payment within thirty days, the dealer shall have no further responsibility to provide a refund under this section. Alternatively, the dealer may elect to offer to replace the used motor vehicle with a comparably priced vehicle, with such adjustment in price as the parties may agree to. The consumer shall not be obligated to accept a replacement vehicle, but may instead elect to receive the refund provided under this section. It shall be an affirmative defense to any claim under this section that:

(a) The malfunction or defect does not substantially impair such value; or

(b) The malfunction or defect is the result of abuse, neglect or unreasonable modifications or alterations of the used motor vehicle.

2. It shall be presumed that a dealer has had a reasonable opportunity to correct a malfunction or defect in a used motor vehicle, if:

(a) The same malfunction or defect has been subject to repair three or more times by the selling or leasing dealer or his agent within the warranty period, but such malfunction or defect continues to exist; or

(b) The vehicle is out of service by reason of repair or malfunction or defect for a cumulative total of fifteen or more days during the warranty period. Said period shall not include days when the dealer is unable to complete the repair because of the unavailability of necessary repair parts. The dealer shall be required to exercise due diligence in attempting to obtain necessary repair parts. Provided, however, that if a vehicle has been out of service for a cumulative total of forty-five days, even if a portion of that time is attributable to the unavailability of replacement parts, the consumer shall be entitled to the replacement or refund remedies provided in this section.

3. The term of any warranty, service contract or repair insurance shall be extended by any time period during which the used motor vehicle is in the possession of the dealer or his duly authorized agent for the purpose of repairing the used motor vehicle under the terms and obligations of said warranty, service contract or repair insurance.

4. The term of any warranty, service contract or repair insurance, and the fifteen day out-of-service period, shall be extended by any time during which repair services are not available to the consumer because of a war, invasion or strike, fire, flood or other natural disaster.

d. Waiver void.

1. Any agreement entered into by a consumer for the purchase or lease of a used motor vehicle which waives, limits or disclaims the rights set forth in this article shall be void as contrary to public policy. Further, if a dealer fails to give the written warranty required by this article, the dealer nevertheless shall be deemed to have given said warranty as a matter of law.

2. Nothing in this section shall in any way limit the rights or remedies which are otherwise available to a consumer under any other law.

3. Notwithstanding paragraph one of this subdivision, this article shall not apply to used motor vehicles sold for, or in the case of a lease where the value of the used motor vehicle as agreed to by the consumer and the dealer which vehicle is the subject of the contract is, less than one thousand five hundred dollars, or to used motor vehicles with over one hundred thousand miles at the time of sale or lease if said mileage is

indicated in writing at the time of sale or lease. Further, this article shall not apply to the sale or lease of classic cars registered pursuant to section four hundred one of the vehicle and traffic law.

e. Time of delivery, location of warranty and notice.

The written warranty provided for in subdivision b of this section and the written notice provided for in subdivision c of this section shall be delivered to the consumer at or before the time the consumer signs the sales or lease contract for the used motor vehicle. The warranty and the notice may be set forth on one sheet or on separate sheets. They may be separate from, attached to, or a part of the sales or lease contract. If they are part of the sales or lease contract, they shall be separated from the other contract provisions and each headed by a conspicuous title.

f. Arbitration and enforcement.

1. If a dealer has established or participates in an informal dispute settlement procedure which complies in all respects with the provisions of part seven hundred three of title sixteen of the code of federal regulations the provisions of this article concerning refunds or replacement shall not apply to any consumer who has not first resorted to such procedure. Dealers utilizing informal dispute settlement procedures pursuant to this subdivision shall insure that arbitrators participating in such informal dispute settlement procedures are familiar with the provisions of this section and shall provide to arbitrators and consumers who seek arbitration a copy of the provisions of this section together with the following notice in conspicuous ten point bold face type:

USED CAR LEMON LAW BILL OF RIGHTS

1. IF YOU PURCHASE A USED CAR FOR MORE THAN ONE THOUSAND FIVE HUNDRED DOLLARS, OR LEASE A USED CAR WHERE YOU AND THE DEALER HAVE AGREED THAT THE CAR'S VALUE IS MORE THAN ONE THOUSAND FIVE HUNDRED DOLLARS, FROM ANYONE SELLING OR LEASING THREE OR MORE USED CARS A YEAR, YOU MUST BE GIVEN A WRITTEN WARRANTY.

2. IF YOUR USED CAR HAS THIRTY-SIX THOUSAND MILES OR LESS, THE WARRANTY MUST EXTEND FOR AT LEAST SIXTY DAYS OR THREE THOUSAND MILES, WHICHEVER COMES FIRST.

3. IF YOUR USED CAR HAS MORE THAN THIRTY- SIX THOUSAND MILES, THE WARRANTY MUST EXTEND FOR AT LEAST THIRTY DAYS OR ONE THOUSAND MILES, WHICHEVER COMES FIRST. CARS WITH OVER ONE HUNDRED THOUSAND MILES ARE NOT COVERED.

4. IF YOUR ENGINE, TRANSMISSION, DRIVE AXLE, BRAKES, RADIATOR, STEERING, ALTERNATOR, GENERATOR, STARTER, OR IGNITION SYSTEM (EXCLUDING THE BATTERY) ARE DEFECTIVE, THE DEALER OR HIS AGENT MUST REPAIR OR, IF HE SO CHOOSES, REIMBURSE YOU FOR THE REASONABLE COST OF REPAIR.

5. IF THE SAME PROBLEM CANNOT BE REPAIRED AFTER THREE OR MORE ATTEMPTS, YOU ARE ENTITLED TO RETURN THE CAR AND RECEIVE A REFUND OF YOUR PURCHASE PRICE, OR OF ALL PAYMENTS MADE UNDER YOUR LEASE CONTRACT, AND OF SALES TAX AND FEES, MINUS A REASONABLE ALLOWANCE FOR ANY DAMAGE NOT ATTRIBUTABLE TO NORMAL USAGE OR WEAR, AND, IN THE CASE OF A LEASE CONTRACT, A CANCELLATION OF ALL FURTHER PAYMENTS YOU ARE OTHERWISE REQUIRED TO MAKE UNDER THE LEASE CONTRACT.

6. IF YOUR CAR IS OUT OF SERVICE TO REPAIR A PROBLEM FOR A TOTAL OF FIFTEEN DAYS OR MORE DURING THE WARRANTY PERIOD YOU ARE ENTITLED TO RETURN THE CAR AND RECEIVE A REFUND OF YOUR PURCHASE PRICE OR ALL PAYMENTS MADE UNDER YOUR LEASE CONTRACT, AND OF SALES TAX AND FEES, MINUS A REASONABLE ALLOWANCE FOR ANY DAMAGE NOT ATTRIBUTABLE TO NORMAL USAGE OR WEAR, AND, IN THE CASE OF A LEASE CONTRACT, A CANCELLATION OF ALL FURTHER PAYMENTS

THE USED VEHICLE LEMON LAW

YOU ARE OTHERWISE REQUIRED TO MAKE UNDER THE LEASE CONTRACT.

7. A DEALER MAY PUT INTO THE WRITTEN WARRANTY CERTAIN PROVISIONS WHICH WILL PROHIBIT YOUR RECOVERY UNDER CERTAIN CONDITIONS; HOWEVER, THE DEALER MAY NOT CAUSE YOU TO WAIVE ANY RIGHTS UNDER THIS LAW.

8. A DEALER MAY REFUSE TO REFUND YOUR PURCHASE PRICE, OR THE PAYMENTS MADE UNDER YOUR LEASE CONTRACT, IF THE PROBLEM DOES NOT SUBSTANTIALLY IMPAIR THE VALUE OF YOUR CAR, OR IF THE PROBLEM IS CAUSED BY ABUSE, NEGLECT, OR UNREASONABLE MODIFICATION.

9. IF A DEALER HAS ESTABLISHED AN ARBITRATION PROCEDURE, THE DEALER MAY REFUSE TO REFUND YOUR PURCHASE PRICE UNTIL YOU FIRST RESORT TO THE PROCEDURE. IF THE DEALER DOES NOT HAVE AN ARBITRATION PROCEDURE, YOU MAY RESORT TO ANY REMEDY PROVIDED BY LAW AND MAY BE ENTITLED TO YOUR ATTORNEY'S FEES IF YOU PREVAIL.

10. AS AN ALTERNATIVE TO THE ARBITRATION PROCEDURE MADE AVAILABLE THROUGH THE DEALER YOU MAY INSTEAD CHOOSE TO SUBMIT YOUR CLAIM TO AN INDEPENDENT ARBITRATOR, APPROVED BY THE ATTORNEY GENERAL. YOU MAY HAVE TO PAY A FEE FOR SUCH AN ARBITRATION. CONTACT YOUR LOCAL CONSUMER OFFICE OR ATTORNEY GENERAL'S OFFICE TO FIND OUT HOW TO ARRANGE FOR INDEPENDENT ARBITRATION.

11. IF ANY DEALER REFUSES TO HONOR YOUR RIGHTS OR YOU ARE NOT SATISFIED BY THE INFORMAL DISPUTE SETTLEMENT PROCEDURE, COMPLAIN TO THE NEW YORK STATE ATTORNEY GENERAL, EXECUTIVE OFFICE, CAPITOL, ALBANY, N.Y. 12224.

2. A dealer shall have up to thirty days from the date of notice by the consumer that the arbitrator's decision has been accepted to comply with the terms of such decision. Provided, however, that nothing contained in this subdivision shall impose any liability on a dealer where a delay beyond the thirty day period is attributable to a consumer who has requested a particular replacement vehicle or otherwise made compliance impossible within said period.

3. Upon the payment of a prescribed filing fee, a consumer shall have the option of submitting any dispute arising under this section to an alternative arbitration mechanism established pursuant to regulations promulgated hereunder by the attorney general. Upon application of the consumer and payment of the filing fee, the dealer shall submit to such alternate arbitration.

Such alternate arbitration shall be conducted by a professional arbitrator or arbitration firm appointed by or under regulations established by the attorney general. Such mechanism shall ensure the personal objectivity of its arbitrators and the right of each party to present its case, to be in attendance during any presentation made by the other party and to rebut such presentation. In all other respects, such alternative arbitration mechanism shall be governed by article seventy-five of the civil practice laws and rules.

The notice required by paragraph one of this subdivision, entitled Used Car Lemon Law Bill of Rights, shall be provided to arbitrators and consumers who seek arbitration under the subdivision.

A dealer shall have thirty days from the date of mailing of a copy of the arbitrator's decision to such a dealer to comply with the terms of such decision. Failure to comply within the thirty day period shall entitle the consumer to recover, in addition to any other recovery to which he may be entitled, a fee of twenty-five dollars for each business day beyond thirty days up to five hundred dollars; provided however, that nothing in this subdivision shall impose any liability on a dealer where a delay beyond the thirty day period is attributable to a consumer who has requested a particular replacement vehicle or otherwise made compliance impossible within said period.

4. In no event shall a consumer who has resorted to an informal dispute settlement procedure be precluded from seeking the rights or remedies available by law.

5. In an action brought to enforce the provisions of this article, the court may award reasonable attorney's fees to a prevailing plaintiff or to a consumer who prevails in any judicial action or proceeding arising out of an arbitration proceeding held pursuant to paragraph three of this subdivision. In the event a prevailing plaintiff is required to retain the services of an attorney to enforce the collection of an award granted pursuant to this section, the court may assess against the dealer reasnoable attorney's fees for services rendered to enforce collection of said award.

6. Any action brought pursuant to this article shall be commenced within four years of the date of original delivery of the used motor vehicle to the consumer.

* WHAT IT MEANS IN SIMPLE ENGLISH:

What all this means in layman's terms is :

1a.) Used car warranties for vehicles purchased with 36,000 miles or less are in effect for 90 days or 4,000 miles - whichever occurs first.

1b.) Used car warranties for vehicles purchased with mileage in excess of 36,000 miles but less than 80,000 miles are in effect for 60 days or 3,000 miles - whichever occurs first.

1c.) Used warranties for vehicles purchased with mileage of 80,000 miles or more, but less than 100,000 miles are in effect for 30 days or 1,000 miles - whichever occurs first.

2.) In the aforementioned time periods (Sections 1a, b & c), the owner must have returned the vehicle to the dealer or notified said dealer of the defect within the allotted time periods.

3.) The warranty should be in writing and must cover repairs (parts and labor) for most engine, transmission, brake, radiator, alternator, starter, and ignition system (battery excluded) components.

4.) The law views any vehicle which has a substantial defect that is not corrected within three attempts by the dealer within a reasonable period of time *or* any vehicle which is out of service due to repair work for a cumulative total of 15 days or more to be a Lemon. This entitles you, the consumer, to a full refund of the purchase price of the vehicle (including the book value of any trade in, all sales tax, license and registration fees) plus - and this is a very important plus - full recovery of all court and attorney's fees. The consumer also has the option to obtain a replacement vehicle of equal value from the dealer as a settlement. A deduction of the refund can be made by the courts for any damage, alteration, or excess mileage on the vehicle. It is important to note that the law states that all outstanding liens on the vehicle must be paid in full prior to the dealer refund to the consumer.

* Other important factors to note are as follows:

1. The new vehicle lemon law, as outlined in Chapter 1, is in effect on any used vehicle that has less than 18,000 miles and is less than two years old. It takes precedence over the used vehicle lemon law and is transferable with the vehicle to the new owner.

THE USED VEHICLE LEMON LAW

2. Any vehicle that is out of service for a cumulative total of 45 days, for any reason(s), (excluding flood, war, etc.) is considered to be a Lemon.

3. Used vehicles sold with a purchase price of less than $1,500.00 are not covered under this law. Small claims would cover any cases that fall below the $1,500.00 threshold.

4. Any vehicles that have 100,000 or more miles are not covered under this law.

* NEW/PENDING AMENDMENTS:

I have added this list which explains the new and pending amendments to the New York State Used Vehicle Lemon Law in an effort to keep this writing as current as possible at the time of its publication. It outlines recent developments in the law that could prove to be of great value for the consumers in New York State. This list represents amendments to the law that have recently been incorporated into the law or are waiting for final approval by the state legislature. They are:

- The law has been updated to define a used motor vehicle as any vehicle that has more than 18,000 miles on the odometer or is more than two years old. This covers any vehicle which is purchased, leased, or transferred to other owners within the aforementioned period. Vehicle mileage and age now become the sole determinant of the vehicle status under the law. The gray area between the New York State New and the New York State Used Vehicle Lemon Law should be effectively eliminated by this change. This is good news for those consumers who have purchased or leased a "demonstrator" vehicle.

- Legal fees incurred by the consumer in an effort to cause a manufacturer or dealer to comply with the arbitrator or court ruling are now covered by the law.

LEMONAID!

- Tougher and easier to follow procedures are being instituted to insure that any vehicle judged to be a lemon comes with a title ''branding'' it as such.

- Lastly, the following extensions of the periods in which a used vehicle is covered have been incorporated

36,000 miles or less - Vehicles will be covered by the law for 90 days or 4,000 miles - whichever comes first.

More than 36,000 miles but less than 80,000 miles - Vehicles will be covered by the law for 60 days or 3,000 miles - whichever comes first.

80,000 miles but less than 100,000 miles - Vehicles will be covered for 30 days or 1,000 miles - whichever comes first.

The reader should know that an arbitration procedure is required in New York State before they can take the case to court if the dealer has such a process in place. So, if you meet the requirements and have the will to fight it out...READ ON!

CHAPTER 3

THE TWO D'S - DOCUMENTATION AND DETERMINATION

To prevail in the lawsuit, the consumer will need two things - a well-documented case that meets the requirements of the Lemon Law, and a determined attitude on the part of the consumer and his attorney(if he has an attorney). Having read only this far, you are probably still unsure of the amount of determination that you will require - or how much you have at the present time... so let's talk about documentation first.

* DOCUMENTATION:

All you need to know is that documentation is any type of written record pertaining to your case that you receive or send during the course of your dealings with the manufacturer and his organization or with any private or government agency. Examples of the type of documentation that you should save for use in the case would be as follows:

-- Original dealer order form issued by the car dealer.

-- Sales receipt for the vehicle issued by the dealer on the day of delivery to you.

-- Warranty books and manuals which came with the vehicle.

-- Work order receipts from the dealer or any agent thereof for service and repairs effected on the vehicle during the first two-year or 18,000 mile period(New Vehicle Lemon Law); or, the first 60-day or 3,000 mile period(Used Vehicle Lemon Law).

-- Receipts/written estimates for any work that is required or was accomplished on the vehicle by your own outside mechanic during the first two-year or 18,000 mile period. (It is usually a good practice to get two separate estimates for any additional work that may be required.)

LEMONAID!

-- Copies of letters which you sent to the dealership, auto manufacturer, government agencies, or consumer groups, which documented your case and complaint. I can't stress strongly enough the need for the claimant to send any and all such correspondence by certified return receipt mail. This provides proof that the document was sent and subsequently received by the proper recipient. Retain all receipts for these mailings.

-- Maintenance record of the vehicle.

Keeping the maintenance record on the vehicle is very important for this reason: during the case, the manufacturer could argue that the defects of the vehicle were the direct result of lack of maintenance or abuse on the part of the consumer. A comprehensive and well-kept maintenance log book, with the related receipts, will be invaluable in refuting any accusations.

An example of what the maintenance log should look like is given below. I used (and still do use) a standard 6 x 9 inch steno note pad. Examples of some of my headers and log entries were as follows:

1984 Pontiac Fiero SE

- Maintenance Log -

Date	Task	Mileage	Cost
8/2/84	Purchased New	00004	$12,681.25
8/2/84	Undercoat & Plates	00004	$111.00
8/3/84	Alarm System	00075	$298.00

DOCUMENTATION AND DETERMINATION

Date	Task	Mileage	Cost
8/7/84	Oil, Filter & Grease	00548	$7.00
8/11/84	Scotch Guard - Int.	00807	$8.00
8/11/84	Splash Guards	00807	$8.00
8/15/84	Oil, Filter & Grease	01062	$7.00
9/18/84	Oil, Filter & Grease	03057	$7.00

I also kept all oil filter receipts and box tops related to the log entries. Some new vehicle owners' manuals have a section in the back which is set up to be used as a maintenance log and you might prefer to do it this way. Either method is sufficient and a definite asset when preparing and fighting the case.

In addition, keep any receipts for alterations or upgrades which are permanent and increase the value of the vehicle. Examples of these are theft alarms, stereos, special wheels, etc. These items are part of the vehicle, and as such, will be considered when the arbitrator or court is determining the dollar amount of the *buy-back judgment.*

* SETTING UP THE SIX PART-FOLDER:

As for organizing all of this documentation, I found that a six-part folder is an invaluable aid. I used a hard cardboard 8-1/2'' x 11'' folder subdivided into six sections, with two folding metal tabs at the top of each section for inserting hole-punched documents. I first used the folder

in my job as a subcontract administrator for a military aircraft manufacturing contractor. It served as a basic recordkeeping tool which was used
during the numerous U.S. Government contract audits that took place
throughout our production runs.

This type of organization has two advantages: 1) As was previously
stated, the six-part folder is a great way to get and stay organized
throughout the duration of the case; 2) It will prove to be an invaluable
tool when it comes time for your lawyer to review and put the case
together. When you go to the arbitrator or lawyer with organized
documentation like this, you are showing them that you are serious about
trying the case and are determined to win.

The important information that I compiled in my six-part folder can
be found in Appendix A. The following is a suggested outline of how
to organize the case paperwork and correspondence:

-- Section 1) "Service records and receipts" - A typewritten narrative
of all service/complaints on the vehicle in conjunction with all the related
receipts and work orders.

-- Section 2) "Correspondence" - In this section I put all the letters that
were sent concerning the case. Note: I once again remind the reader to
send all correspondence by certified return receipt mail. This may seem
repetitive, but I feel it is essential to remind you so that you comply with
the law and maximize your chance of success.

-- Section 3) "Supporting documents and research" - In this section of
the six-part folder I placed other material that pertained either to the
vehicle itself or to the arbitration or court case.

-- Section 4) "State Agencies and Consumer Groups" - I kept all
documentation that I acquired from state agencies and consumer groups
in this section. These documents proved useful in both the arbitration
and legal proceedings of the case.

DOCUMENTATION AND DETERMINATION

-- Section 5) "Documentation" - This section contains legal documents that are self-explanatory.

-- Section 6) "Arbitration " - This section was used to file all information and documentation pertaining to the arbitration proceedings.

To briefly summarize this chapter - get yourself organized from the start. Keep complete and comprehensive records of everything that happened so you can build a well-documented case that you will ultimately win. Good recordkeeping and documentation will prove invaluable to both you and your lawyer. In short, your determination to keep good records is equally as important as your determination to win. Remember: DETERMINATION & DOCUMENTATION ARE DEFINITELY THE WINNING COMBINATION !

CHAPTER 4

BUILDING YOUR CASE

* WARRANTY REQUIREMENTS:

The first chapter of this book outlined the minimum requirements which you must meet to qualify under the Lemon Law. For new vehicles purchased in the state of New York the requirements are, briefly:

Four unsuccessful repair attempts on a substantial vehicle defect within a 2-year or 18,000 mile period.

OR

Loss of vehicle (vehicle out of service) for a cumulative total of thirty (30) days within a 2-year or 18,000 mile period.

The used vehicle requirements are somewhat similar but have shorter mileage and time requirements (see Chapter 2).

In order to prove that you have met the requirements, you must build the case in a step by step manner, documenting each step. If you bring the vehicle back to the dealership or any authorized agent of the auto manufacturer -- get a copy of the work order. Calculate and keep a record of the number of days that the vehicle was out of service. Make sure that you use *exactly the same* description of the vehicle defect every time you bring it in for a repeat repair attempt. Also, make sure that the same terminology appears on the dealer's or agent's work order.

* THE MANUFACTURER'S ORGANIZATION:

If you feel that you are getting unsatisfactory results on the repair attempts -- start to traverse your way up the dealership's organizational ladder. First, inform the service manager of your plight. If that doesn't yield positive results, move on to the manager -- then on to the owner of the dealership if need be. I suggest that you keep a small log on what was discussed, with whom, on what date, and what resulted or was agreed upon. To further build your case, send a certified return/receipt letter to the owner of the dealership, outlining your complaints and reviewing the vehicles' service history. This letter should also reference what was agreed (if anything) during your communication with him.

Still no relief in sight? OK, don't get frustrated. Get the warranty book that was given to you when you purchased the car.

Somewhere in the back of the book is a section entitled "Owner Assistance." This section gives you phone numbers for the manufacturer's customer service representatives in both the zone and central offices. Call the zone office, repeat your story and follow it up with a certified letter. If this yields no result, which is quite possible, follow the same procedure with the central office -- call, repeat your story and follow it up with a certified letter. The receipt that you get for the certified letter shows the fee that you paid to the post office to have it sent. Keep tabs on all these costs and add them to your claim for legal fees. It's also a good idea to keep a record of these conversations in a "telephone log." Remember, all these efforts on your part constitute building a case (and as such should be stored in the appropriate section of the six-part folder.)

If you have run all the traps mentioned thus far, but fruitlessly -- let me first say that I fully know how you feel. Remember, I've already gone down this road. However, there is a further course of action that can be taken; a course that will take you to victory. So take heart -- there is a light at the end of the tunnel.

I am going to assume at this point that you have reached the point where you are completely convinced that you: 1) have purchased a lemon; 2) Have met all the requirements that your state requires in order to legally consider the vehicle a lemon (new or used); 3) Have everything documented as outlined in this text; 4) Are determined to go the distance.

BUILDING YOUR CASE

When all these conditions are met, you are ready to take the first step to obtain relief under the statutes of the Lemon Law. The following chapters outline what will take place at third-party arbitration, and how you should prepare. So take a deep breath and read on!

CHAPTER 5

GUIDANCE AND AIDS - PREARBITRATION

Arbitration is a process by which the consumer and the auto manufacturer meet to plead their cases before a third party. Keep in mind that most states require by law that you go through the arbitration process first, before pursuing the case in court. The reader should know that the judgment of the arbitrator is binding on the manufacturer, but not on the consumer.

What this means is that if the consumer agrees with the arbitrator's decision/remedy, then the manufacturer must comply. If, on the other hand, the consumer does not agree with the arbitrator's ruling, he/she still has the option to pursue the case further in court. But be aware that the consumer gives up the right to pursue the matter in court if he/she agrees to go along with the remedy that the arbitrator has prescribed.

You are about 80% prepared for the arbitration hearing if you already have your case documented as outlined previously. All you really have to do is to present your case from the narrative that you have prepared and filed in Section I of the six-part folder. Needless to say, this narrative should be backed up by copies of all receipts, work orders, and estimates referred to in the narrative. The consumer should only submit copies of the receipts, retaining all originals for himself.

* THE STATE ATTORNEY GENERAL'S OFFICE:

Now let's get down to the remaining 20% of the information that you should be familiar with and have on hand prior to and during the arbitration proceedings. The first place to start is your local State Attorney General's office. The one that I went to was extremely helpful. They gave me a certain amount of guidance in addition to a pamphlet which explained the Lemon Law and my rights in plain English. Excerpts of the latest pamphlet are reproduced for the reader's reference in Appendix B at the back of this book.

LEMONAID!

Once you have contacted your local Attorney General's office, you should then contact the designated agency which runs the arbitration hearings in your state. If your state has a Lemon Law and requires an arbitration hearing prior to litigation, your local Attorney General's office can provide you with a list of designated agencies. You should be aware that different auto manufacturers have different agencies even though they are located in the same state. This agency (in my case the Better Business Bureau) will have the proper complaint forms for you to complete to get the arbitration hearing started. In addition, they should also have an informative pamphlet which outlines what you have to do to prepare yourself for the hearing, and what your rights are under the law in your particular state.

The New York State Lemon Law Arbitration Regulations can be found in Appendix C. The information provided in Appendices B and C should prove invaluable to the consumer.

* LIBRARY PUBLICATIONS AND ARTICLES:

The last place to gather information for the arbitration hearing is your local public library. Your local law library (usually at a State or City College/University) can provide you with a copy of the law itself (if it isn't in the Attorney General's pamphlet). You may even find articles which address the particular defect in the automobile that you are experiencing, as well as articles which tell of other consumers who fought and won.

An article which I felt was helpful in my preparation for the arbitration was in the November 1983 issue of "Consumer Reports" and was entitled *"Winning Through Arbitration."* This article contained many valuable pointers. A copy of the article can be obtained by mailing $3.00 to Ms. Wendy Wintman at Consumers Union, 256 Washington Street, Mount Vernon, N.Y. 10553. I view it as "required reading" for anyone getting ready for an arbitration hearing in New York State.

GUIDANCE AND AIDS - PREARBITRATION

My research in the library turned up an article in the August 1985 issue of "Popular Mechanics" which was entitled *"Fiero Cracked Block Problems."* In it the author, Mr. Shultz, outlined the exact defect that I experienced with my 1984 Fiero. I couldn't believe it when I read a more recent article in the July 1990 issue of the same magazine in which a reader wrote about his 1984 Fiero's oil getting "yellow and milky." Written by Mike Allen, it illustrated exactly where the cracks in the block occur. I certainly can sympathize with that Fiero owner and hope that he didn't wind up with the vehicle that I gave back to GM !

It is at this point that I should talk about a recent development in the law that will encourage the reader to pursue his or her case with even more optimism than I had. As you know, having read Chapter 1, the new vehicle lemon law in New York calls for the consumer to go through an arbitration hearing prior to taking the case to court.

The State Attorney General's office in New York has made the law tougher than it was when I went through arbitration. The proceedings as outlined under the previous law were not as consumer-oriented as they are today. Today, all applications for arbitration must be filed with the State Attorney General's office, where they are screened to see if they meet the statutes of the Lemon Law. If they do, the case is then referred to an independent organization called the American Arbitration Association, or AAA. The AAA charges the consumer an arbitration fee of $200.00 which is refundable if the consumer wins. The real beauty of this new development is that the entire procedure only takes about 45 days.

The results of this program have been excellent as relates to the consumer in New York State. In 1988, consumers prevailed in 60.5% of the cases and received close to $18 million dollars in awards plus settlements. Results for 1989 were 66% of consumers recouping close to $17 million for awards plus settlements. New York State consumers have recovered in excess of $50 million (as of 12/31/89) since the program was instituted in 1987.

LEMONAID!

This means that if you purchased, leased and or registered the vehicle in New York State, you should not have to retain a lawyer and go to court like I did -- although you might want to consult with one before you proceed with your case. Remember that my case took place prior to the inception of the AAA procedure. This procedure is described in detail in Chapter 6.

The bottom line here is that if the vehicle was purchased or leased in New York State, or any state which has an independent arbitration board such as the AAA, it would be in the consumer's best interest to go to arbitration. I would strongly urge the reader to go to or contact the State Attorney General's office in order to initiate the procedure. It would take a lot less time and effort to obtain a legal remedy under the Lemon Law than it would for the average consumer to go out and earn the money required to purchase a replacement vehicle. Under this system, the consumer should definitely prevail if he or she has a solid and well documented case. The next chapter is written to help the reader prepare to go through the arbitration process.

CHAPTER 6

THE ARBITRATION PROCEDURE

*ARBITRATION WITH THE AMERICAN ARBITRATION ASSOCIATION:

Your local State Attorney General's office can be used to locate the agency you require for the arbitration hearing. As was previously discussed, consumers in New York State should go through arbitration with the American Arbitration Association (AAA). In certain states some automobile manufacturers have set up their own arbitration boards, but my lawyer does not recommend this route. A representative of the Attorney General's office or the arbitration agency will be able to counsel you and provide an information packet which should include an outline of the proceeding and an arbitration complaint form. This form is to be filled out and returned to the issuing agency for review and subsequent scheduling of the arbitration hearing. The information packet advises you of your rights and explains what you will be required to do in order to prepare for the hearing. An outline of how the proceeding will be conducted should also be included. This information is both valuable and useful to the consumer and should be read carefully, several times, prior to the hearing.

When it comes time to plead your case at the arbitration hearing, show up on time, and state your case as clearly and calmly as possible. You should have copies of the narrative from which you will read for both the arbitrator and the auto manufacturer's representative so they can follow along. Try not to be nervous or angry. The arbitrator will outline in the beginning how the procedure will be run and what is required of both parties. Once again, just follow the instructions that you are given, stay calm, and plead your case. Remember, "those that anger you, defeat you." And we both know that you are not going to be defeated. Make sure to emphasize that you have experienced four unsuccessful repair attempts for a serious vehicle defect and/or a loss of the vehicle for a total of 30 or more days during the first two-year/18,000-mile period. If you are going through a used vehicle arbitration, refer to Chapter 2 for number of repair attempts and out-of-service requirements. Get in there and give it your best effort!

You will be notified of the arbitrator's decision by mail several weeks after the hearing. The notification will include a form which you have to fill out, sign, and return, indicating whether or not you accept the decision. Keep in mind that acceptance on your part prevents you from pursuing the matter in court any further. Be absolutely certain that you are 100 percent satisfied with the decision and remedy prescribed by the arbitration agency prior to your signing of the form. By signing this form you accept the arbitrator's decision. If you do not accept the decision, you must indicate so on the form, sign it, and mail it back to the agency.

*NEW YORK STATE SALES TAX REFUND PROCEDURE:

Remember that if you win and opt for the cash refund settlement, you are entitled to a refund of the New York State Sales Tax that was paid on the vehicle. A form for the tax refund must be filled out and submitted to the New York State Department of Taxation and Finance Sales Tax Refund Unit , W.A. Harriman Campus , Albany, N.Y. The refund will be calculated at the tax rate that was paid at the time the vehicle was originally purchased times the amount of money (less legal fees) that was awarded to the consumer for the vehicle. My New York State tax refund came to $948.75 and took about five weeks to obtain. This refund represented the lion's share of the $973.09 that I paid when I originally purchased the Fiero. A copy of the refund check can be found at the end of this chapter.

It is my true hope that any reader who accepts the decision of the arbitrator receives an ample remedy and is ultimately happy with the final outcome. If this is in fact the case, you need not read any further -- Good Luck to you -- and please pass this book on to someone who might require it.

THE ARBITRATION PROCEDURE

If on the other hand, you are one of those people who are dissatisfied with the decision or are at this point in time unsure of what to do -- read on to find out the next step in the process. Chapters 7 thru 10 were written for those people like myself, whom I feel are in the majority (prior to the AAA) or who are presently in a state that does not have an AAA-type organization. Take heart -- you are not alone. Your plight is the reason why I wrote this book.

If you have not yet read consumer advocate Ralph Nader's book **Unsafe At Any Speed,** now is the time to read it. Mr. Nader's book shows how the auto manufacturers have been trying to cover up their mistakes and manipulate the system through the years. Most people remember this book as the one that killed the General Motors Chevrolet Corvair, but it is so much more. For example ,it gives insight into safety cover ups and how manufacturers lobbied against safety legislation.

You will definitely view the automobile manufacturers and your own automobile in a different light once you have read Nader's book. It shows just how far the automobile manufacturers were forced to go to improve the safety and environmental standards of their cars from the 40's through the 80's. In my opinion it also points out just how far they still must be forced to go(through legislation).

My hope is that **LemonAid!** will do for the consumer's *financial* safety what Nader's book has done for the consumer's *physical* safety. Once again, I strongly urge you to read Mr. Nader's book. It will put your plight in a totally different perspective and give you valuable insight into the manufacturers' attempts to pacify disgruntled consumers.

Getting back on track, if you have come this far without obtaining a satisfactory result, then the following chapter will outline the next step. This step is the one where you locate and retain a lawyer in order to start the court proceedings; proceedings which will be presided over by a lawyer and be bound to follow the statutes of the Lemon Law of your state.

LEMONAID!

State of New York

No. 01372610

COMPTROLLER STATE OF NEW YORK - REFUND ACCOUNT

MAY 17, 1990

KNOW YOUR ENDORSER

01372610
50-62
213
P

PAY TO THE
ORDER OF

┌ 20150
S   20150 ST
ANDREW A FAGLIO

$948.75

20150   ST55454

$948.75

Edward V. Regan
EDWARD V. REGAN
STATE COMPTROLLER

STATE COMPTROLLER

SIGNATURE OF THE
STATE COMPTROLLER
IS THE ONLY ONE
REQUIRED ON THIS CHECK

Union National
A MIDLANTIC BANK

⑈013726⑈0⑈ ⑈0213006⑈4⑈ ⑈605009072⑈8⑈

Illustration A: Refund Check - New York State Sales Tax

CHAPTER 7

KID DYNAMITE - SECURING THE RIGHT LAWYER

* LOCAL BAR ASSOCIATION:

If you are like I was, and do not have a lawyer whom you deal with on a regular basis, you will have to locate one, preferably an attorney who is familiar with consumer law. Your best bet in this instance is to contact your local Bar Association; the phone number in your area can be obtained by using the telephone directory. A representative of the Bar Association will listen to your situation and furnish you with the names and phone numbers of several lawyers who specialize in this type of case. It is then your perogative to telephone and discuss the merits of your case with a lawyer. Once you have discussed the issues of the case and cost, you must make a decision.

The decision you must make at this time is two fold: Are you willing to risk the time and money that is necessary to pursue the case from this point until the end? And, which lawyer do you chose? The first decision is a personal one which basically depends on what you conclude after listening to what the attorney has said about the merits of the case, and about the time and money expenditures that will be involved. The second decision isn't that difficult once the first one has been made. You should retain a lawyer who you feel is economical, capable, aggressive, and familiar with the technical workings of an automobile. Previous experience with the Lemon Law would also be desirable. The best bet would be to retain a lawyer on a "contingency basis," which means that the lawyer gets paid only if he or she wins the case for you.

My lawyer couldn't have been better, and I am not saying that just because he won the case (although it sure didn't hurt). His name is George J. Haggerty. George has all the winning attributes one needs to be a succesful attorney -- he is bright, aggressive, and he knows the law. In addition George worked in the State Attorney General's office while attending St. Johns University Law School. Lastly, and equally impor- tant, was the fact that George's family was in the automobile repair business for years, George had an extensive working knowledge of automobiles.

I really can not say enough about George and his legal assistant, Janet. They kept me informed and kept moving the case along. George refused to give the General Motors lawyers an inch; he would not be intimidated. His determination to go the distance with me was a major factor in our victory over the largest automobile manufacturer in the world. So if you think that you can do it without a lawyer or with just "any old lawyer" - better think again. Anyone who is of that conviction doesn't know the legal system and has never had the good fortune to come across a lawyer like George.

The following is a brief outline (in English) of what George had to do to proceed with my case. While it is not absolutely necessary to know all the exact details, it is helpful to at least have a working knowledge of what is going on in order to be able to monitor how well your case and your lawyer are progressing.

1) Summons and Complaint - This is the first legal step taken in which your attorney outlines your case and sends it to the manufacturer's representatives. This provides notice to the manufacturer that a law suit has been filed in which the manufacturer is named as the defendant and the basis for that suit. The Summons and Complaint, in effect, initiates your lawsuit.

2) Answer - The manufacturer has thirty to ninety days to review and answer your initial summons and complaint. You can usually count on them to reply with several reasons why they disagree with your claim(s).

3) Particularize - In this step, you will be asked to supply copies of all bills, work orders, and receipts which back up your story.

4) Examination Before Trial (EBT) - Also referred to as a "Deposition." Here the representatives of both sides meet in an effort to establish the parameters of the trial. They will lay out the evidence

each side will present and formulate the points of law for the court to consider.

The "EBT" can also be done in written form. Each side submits a written answer to each of the questions that will be raised at trial. This is known as an "Interrogatory," and is the method that was used in my case with the Fiero.

5) Pretrial Conference(s) - At this point in the legal process opposing parties present their respective cases for review by the judge or his assistant, in an effort to settle the case out of court. It is the last step taken prior to the selection of the jury.

My case was settled at this point. My lawyer met with the representatives of GM before the judge to review the case. It was agreed that I should recoup 97% of the purchase price of the vehicle, plus a $2,000 award to my attorney for legal fees. I felt that this was an equitable solution due to the fact that at this point the vehicle was well over two years old and had mileage in excess of twelve thousand on it. In all fairness, I still feel that my lawyer deserved a higher award for all of the time and effort that he had to put into winning this case for me.

6) Trial - This is the last step if all else fails . It is my understanding, however, that the overwhelming majority of these cases rarely go to trial.

My case did not go to a trial in court. Because the merits of the case were plainly in my favor the judge basically told the General Motors lawyers during a pretrial hearing, that if it did go to trial, he would rule in my favor for a total of $13,500.00. At this point, the General Motors lawyers felt that it would be best to pay the money rather than lose in court and set a legal precedent. It was the greatest feeling to have them tow that LEMON away, and then go to the bank to deposit the check!

LEMONAID!

* LET YOUR ATTORNEY DECIDE THE MERITS OF YOUR CASE:

A few words about what happens during this part of the journey to victory. You will find that the people around you, both family and friends, all have very definite opinions as to what you should or should not do. And lucky you - they are all willing to give you these pearls of wisdom for free! The one piece of advice I feel obligated to give here is: Make up your own mind. After all, it is your car, your time, and your money. Don't base your decision on what other people have to say. There were plenty of people telling me to "go for it" and plenty of people who were telling me that I was crazy and didn't have a chance of winning. Keep the decision making process between you and your lawyer, where it belongs.

I must say that for the most part I was pretty lucky; I had most of my family and friends behind me 100%. However, there were still some people around me that were predicting that I was going to lose. I can even recall reading a few articles in the local newspapers which told stories of people who had fought and lost. These were not terribly encouraging to me at the time, but something caught my eye as I looked through the rest of the paper. I saw many new car advertisements, and I couldn't help but wonder - Would the newspapers run articles that would in effect "go against their pocketbooks"? What do you think?

That's why, whenever you get or hear discouraging news -- check whether the source of "expert" information has a financial interest in the automobile manufacturer , and then judge the merits of the information accordingly. What I am saying here is that no matter what you choose to do in this life, there will always be people ("experts") around who will tell you in no uncertain terms why you can not reach your goal. My advice is DON'T LISTEN TO THEM -- be your own person -- make up your own mind. At the very least, if you decide to do something and it turns out to be a mistake - at least it will be YOUR mistake and not somebody else's.

CHAPTER 8

VICTORY!

* THE GREATEST FEELING - TIME TO CELEBRATE:

As in any other protracted battle, victory is the ultimate goal and reward. Let's face it, nobody likes to feel that they are being taken advantage of by a person or company. This is especially true in a case that involves the second largest purchase that most people make in their lifetimes. My victory over General Motors Corporation was not only a test of my own convictions, but also a test of the legal system in this country. I really wanted to see for myself if the "little guy" had a fair shot at beating the "big guy" in court. The answer was obviously a resounding YES!

I was not alone in this fight and neither are you. A list of the cases of the consumers who have fought and won can be obtained through either the arbitration organization or the State Attorney General's Office.

The copy of the check that I received in conjunction with the picture that follows are proof positive that the system is alive and well. Somebody once said that you can't argue with success. Well success in my case was the victory that I was able to obtain over the General Motors Corporation through the legal system. If you have any doubts, just take a look at the checks and picture on the following page.

Illustration B: My car is towed away.

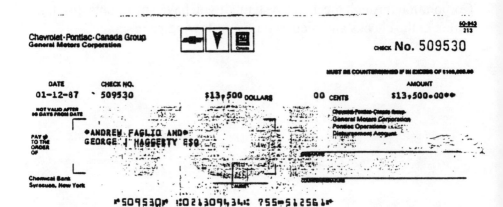

Illustration C: Refund check - General Motors

CHAPTER 9

WHAT IS WRONG WITH THE LAW IN ITS PRESENT FORM

*TOUGHER LAWS ARE NECESSARY

I feel that even though the New York State Lemon Law is good in its present form, three improvements should be made and adopted by all fifty states. The three improvements deal with time and money.

First, the law should present the consumer with a faster means of obtaining a remedy than is presently offered. In New York State this is now being accomplished by the AAA. My fight lasted 18 months from beginning to end-- entirely too long. **Recent improvements in the New York State laws have closed this gap to approximately 45 days.**

* ADDITIONAL AWARD TO COVER REIMBURSEMENT OF ALL LEGAL FEES:

In addition to a faster turnaround time I would also recommend that the law allow the consumer's attorney to collect a fee greater than the $2,000.00 presently provided for. I feel that my attorney deserved much more especially taking into consideration the amount of time and effort that he expended in winning the case. More lawyers would be willing to pursue consumer cases such as mine if more money were awarded for legal fees.

In this way, the courts would strengthen the existing law and prevent car companies from trying to drive a wedge between the consumer and the consumer's attorney by offering either one less money than they deserve.

Lastly, the backlog of cases is prohibitive for the consumer seeking a swift remedy in states that do not offer AAA arbitration as an alternative. This backlog causes many consumers to think twice about bringing a manufacturer to court.

LEMONAID!

* IMPROVEMENTS WOULD BE BENEFICIAL TO ALL:

Tougher New and Used Car Lemon Laws passed in all fifty states are necessary. The new laws must provide for rapid processing of consumer cases. Also, ample awards for the plaintiffs' attorneys would result in better representation for the consumer. More people winning would result in more costs for the automobile companies. Do you know what happens when something costs the automobile companies more money? They wake up and take notice of it -- it's a great way to get their attention. Increased legal costs directly related to the quality of their products and services will cause these automobile manufacturers to reevaluate their quality control procedures. This can only benefit you - the consumer.

In order to ensure that automobile manufacturers take notice of the consumer, each state must enact a Lemon Law with substance. The Federal Government should do its part by disallowing the auto manufacturers any tax break that relates to loss of revenue from lawsuits that involve quality or safety defects due to their negligence. Lemon Laws have been written to protect the consumer on a state level -- Federal laws should be written to protect the consumer/tax payer on a national level. There's no doubt in my mind that this two-pronged approach will wake up the auto manufacturers. Hit them hard in the pocketbook and you'll see how fast they'll sit up and take notice.

CHAPTER 10

SMALL CLAIMS COURT

* CAVALIER PROBLEMS

This last chapter contains events which, if they weren't so tragic, could be considered comical. Looking back on it now I guess it is rather funny. So let me relate to you how my brand new 1987 Chevrolet Cavalier RS quickly turned into another lemon.

So there I was, winning a protracted court battle in which General Motors Corporation was forced to refund 97% of the purchase price of the car, pay my lawyer, and tow away the vehicle. Conscious of the state of the economy I went out and purchased a brand new 1987 Chevy Cavalier RS manufactured in the United States.

I had the car about three months when I took off a half day from work in order for the Pontiac Dealer to send a flat-bed down to pick up the Fiero. A friend of mine met me at my house with his camera and thus the picture that you see at the back of Chapter 8. I felt that it would be an appropriate gesture in light of what I went through. They gave me a Lemon, so I felt it only proper to give them one back!

Well, all in all it was a good day for me -- I had the check and General Motors had the Fiero. Case closed, right? Not quite. While I was dropping off my friend at his house, he said that he thought that he smelled something burning in the Cavalier. I dismissed it as an odor coming in from the outside of the car. As it turned out, the smell was a shorted connector on the steering column of my car which resulted in the failure of my headlights the next day.

I called the dealer and had to wait eight days for the next available appointment. So on the very day that the old story ended, a new one began. In order to survive the eight day wait, I put the high beams on and electrically disconnected the two inboard lamp units.

I dropped the car off eight days later and was told that it would be ready for me that evening. I called the dealership late in the day to confirm that the car was ready. The service manager told me that the car was repaired and that I could come down and pick it up. When I got to the dealership, they told me that they mistook my name for another customer's and that my car had not been repaired. I was informed that they would repair it first thing in the morning. This did not please me in the least. What made matters ten times worse is that the engine started to race on the way home, which caused the car to accelerate, out of control. My first thought was that I didn't remember ordering cruise control on the car. The second thought that came into my mind was that I had a Chevy Cavalier that thought it was an Audi 5000!

At this point I was totally disgusted and couldn't believe that I was experiencing such major problems with another brand new General Motors product. When I returned the vehicle to the dealership the next morning, they repaired the shorted connector which returned the head-lights to full operational status. This made me feel that I now could at least see what I was going to crash into if the car decided to accelerate out of control again at night. The people at the dealership told me that they checked for the idle problem and could find nothing wrong. I must have the "magic touch," because the engine started to idle at about 2300 RPMS (more than twice the normal idle speed) as soon as I started the car.

Now started the repair procedure that I call the "R&R " routine. That is, when they don't know what is wrong. They just Remove and Replace components on your car until the problem goes away. The fun part is when they come up with the highly technical explanation of what was wrong and how they fixed it. At this point I must inform you not to be too upset with the fact that you don't know what they are talking about. You can take comfort in the fact that they don't know either.

This situation grows out of the fact that Ph.D.s design the vehicles; MBA's run the factories; and high school graduates repair them.

Getting back to my repair -- they removed and replaced the Manifold Absolute Pressure Module and the problem remained. They removed and replaced the oxygen sensor and the problem remained. Finally, somebody said that it was probably the Idle Air Control Module on the fuel injector unit. They couldn't remove and replace this because there weren't any available in stock. So I was forced to take the car out of the dealership with the engine racing and wait for them to order the part.

I drove the vehicle for two weeks in this condition, when suddenly and without warning, the car started to accelerate on me while I was trying to slow down on the exit ramp of an expressway. I was forced to engage the clutch and come to a panic stop in order to avoid a collision. At this point the engine was racing erratically. I did my best to nurse the car home. The next morning I started the car and observed that the engine was still racing. At this point, I felt that I had enough and went out and rented a car in order to commute to and from work. I made several phone calls at work to both Chevrolet and the dealership. They agreed to tow the car from my house to the dealership once the part I needed was shipped from the warehouse.

The car was towed from my house to the dealership some time later when the part became available. The part only cost $73.00. All this danger, inconvenience and expense for the lack of a lousy 73-buck part. I was told that the dealer would repair my car the next day.

When I called to inquire about the availability of the car the following day, I was told by the switchboard operator at the dealership that I could not be hooked up with the service area due to a "power failure." I called back several times that day and the following day only to get the same "power failure" explanation.

LEMONAID!

To this day I don't know what possessed me to not believe the power failure excuse. I can remember thinking to myself, "My luck -- the place burned down with my car in it." With this thought in mind, I called the local firehouse to inquire about any recent fires and you guessed it, the place went on fire with my car inside!

At this point, I rushed down to the dealership and saw that although dirty, my car was still intact. Well, it took them two weeks to repair and return the car to me, at which time I was totally disgusted and left with a rental car bill of $353.00. Once again I contacted the dealership and Chevrolet in an effort to obtain a reimbursement for the rental fees that were incurred through no fault of my own.

Once again I was sent the standard "Sorry, but it's not COMPANY POLICY" form letter as an answer to my reimbursement requests. The reader should understand a very important point here: What company policy states and what the LAW allows are often not the same nor even remotely related. The law often entitles the consumer to a lot more than "company policy." Make sure that you know and understand your rights under the law and then pursue them in order to obtain any money or services owed to you by the car companies as prescribed by LAW. A light should go on in the consumer's head from now on whenever he or she hears the phrase "not company policy" in this or any situation.

* SMALL CLAIMS COURT: PROCEDURE AND RESULT:

I was tired of the standard run around that I was getting, so I put everything in writing and filed suit against the Chevrolet Motor Division of General Motors in small claims court. Small claims court fees came to a whopping total of $4.89. When the case came up, the General Motor's lawyers didn't show up and I pleaded my case in the form of an inquest. An inquest is a one-sided case presided over by the judge in the courtroom where the plaintiff has to prove liability and damages. I was able to prove at the inquest that the vehicle was delivered to me with a latent defect for which the manufacturer was liable. Proof of damages was submitted in the form of the receipt for the car rental, the registered letter to Chevrolet, and the court fees. The judge heard my case and ruled in my favor for the full amount of all my bills -- $358.68. Once again, I received a check from General Motors, a copy of which is at the end of this chapter .

This second victory proves several things. One, that General Motors Corporation was still backing defective products with defective service. Two, that "It's not company policy" statements have nothing to do with what the consumer is entitled to under the law. Three, that our system is still alive and well. It allows the little guy to beat the big guy in a court of law when he is in the right--WITH OR WITHOUT THE HELP OF A LAWYER.

Going to small claims court is a very easy matter. It is basically a "Peoples Court" without cameras or Judge Wapner. New York State presently has a $2,000 claim cutoff limit. So if your damages (with receipts as back up) total to less than the allowable limit in your particular state, you can go to your local courthouse and fill out the proper form in order to initiate the processing of your case in small claims court. You will be required to pay a nominal fee of $5.58 ($4.89 in my case) as a registration cost, but take heart, the court will reimburse you for it when you win your case. Be sure to obtain, read, and follow all of the instructions that are contained in the small claims court's information pamphlet.

The reader can treat the procedure of going to small claims court the same as preparing for an arbitration hearing; so document the case as outlined in Chapter 4 and follow through with the instructions that are given in Chapter 6. Needless to say, I had no problem in preparing and winning this case in small claims. At this point in time I was well versed in the procedure. In addition, this Cavalier case was minor as compared to the one that I had to fight with the Fiero.

After reading this chapter, the consumer must conclude that the "system" in this country is alive and well and that it is up to the consumer citizen to use it in order to enforce and preserve it!

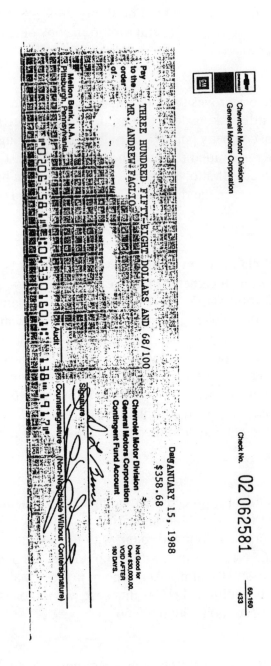

Illustration D: Refund Check - Small Claims Court

CONCLUSION

What does the reader have to gain from my experience? Several things. He or she should know that they are not alone in their struggle; many have fought and prevailed in the past and many more are sure to follow (hopefully with the aid of this book). Also, the legal system is alive and well for the consumer who has a viable case and a good lawyer, coupled with the documentation and determination to win.

Take the manufacturer of a defective car to arbitration or to court. It is the only way that car companies will begin to listen. It is the only way to make things change. Do what the car companies are betting and hoping that you wouldn't do -- TAKE THEM TO COURT! When the consumers begin to cost the car companies as much time and money as they are costing the consumer by producing Lemons every year, maybe the manufacturer will begin to listen and hopefully to improve products and services. Improvements which are reflected in QUALITY design, QUALITY materials, QUALITY manufacturing, QUALITY testing, and QUALITY service.

If you don't think that these methods are effective, just look at General Motors Corporation's track record over the recent past. They have effectively lost 7% of their market share over the past eight years. Needless to say, it came as no surprise to me when I heard on the news that General Motors was shutting down the Fiero production line on September 1, 1988. I guess that the consumer sent a clear message to General Motors by showing them that there wouldn't be a demand for defective products.

In closing, the only advice I can give is to follow the path I chose for myself -- which in recent years has become much faster and easier. If you are experiencing the types of difficulties with your new automobile and its manufacturer as those described in this book, then my advice to you is simply: *Go to ARBITRATION and if necessary to COURT.*

And remember, the moral of this story is:

When life hands you a Lemon...make LemonAid!

APPENDIX A

Excerpts from the Six-Part Folder

APPENDIX A

I chose to only include Sections 1 and 5 from my Six-Part Folder in this Appendix. These two sections of the folder contain my repair records, legal material and correspondence. I feel that the information and examples contained herein will prove to be the most valuable to the consumer.

SIX PART FOLDER - SECTION I

I used this section of the six part folder to store all of my receipts and workorders. The first three pages are basically a log or summary of what transpired during the case with the receipts and workorders as backup. It enabled me to review at a glance all of the events as related to dates, mileage, and amount of days that the vehicle was out of service.

Pontiac Account #
5 2427P

Vehicle I.D. # - 1G2AF37R5EP297911

Purchased New - ~~$12,681.25~~ $12,747.54
Alarm System - 297.69

Invoice Number - N4815 dated 8/2/84

Date	Work Order Number	Mileage	Narrative	Number of Days
9/26/84	W5890	3,988	Defective steering damper replaced.	1
2/7/85	W7666	8,972	1st complaint that engine was missing at idle. Dealer replaced one ignition wire (#4 plug wire).	1
2/11/85	W7690	9,015	2nd complaint that engine was missing at idle. Dealer replaced #1,2,3 ignition wires. Poor workmanship wires poorly routed over intake manifold, all wire looms broken. Timing set to TDC instead of 8° BTC; idle set to 1,150 RPMs instead of 950. (Band-aid fix).	1
2/21/85	W08051	9,642	3rd complaint that engine was missing at idle. Dealer installed an injector. Vehicle out of service for 11 days waiting for parts (2/22/85 thru3/4/85).	11
3/25/85	W08416	10,600	4th complaint that engine was missing at idle. Dealer told me that the engine was not missing. The idle was set at 1,100 RPMs instead of 950; timing set to 12° BTC instead of 8° BTC. (Band-aid fix #2) When I picked up the vehicle it was still missing and demonstrated said condition to the service manager.	1
3/6/85	W08121	9,824	Dealer replaced defective radiator overflow tank.	1
4/18/85	BBB Code 40121	10,800	Complaint registered with the Better Business Bureau so that arbitration date could be set.	
4/19/85			Retained legal consul.	

v

4/22/85	44611	11,000	Took vehicle to an independent certified mechanic.	1
			Problem diagnosed as a bad timing gear. Work Order 44611 Charge: $81.18	
4/26/85	WO9059	12,223	5thcomplaint of engine missing. Vehicle returned to dealer for diagnosis by District Service Manager. Result-Front portion of engine has to be disassemblied at a future date so that problem can be assessed further.	1
5/2/85	WO9141	12,310	6th Complaint of engine missing. Problem diagnosed as a porous engine block, The engine coolant is mixing with the engine oil. Water in the oil. Dealer offered to replace the block. I refused on the grounds that the car is a lemon and that the dealer is not capable of doing an adequate job. This is witnessed by the fact that previous visits to the dealer resulted in shoddy workmanship and band aid fixes.	13
6/20/85	WO9873	12,400	Electric Radiator cooling fan motor "shorted out" resulting in the engine overheating and the melting of the fan blade assembly.	12

7th complaint of engine missing.
Vehicle out of service 6/20/85 thru
7/2/85. I rented two Hertz cars
for 7 out of the 12 days.
Hertz Bill # 63786979-4 $ 105.80
           # 63787050-5   101.54
                      $ 207.34

TO DATE: Lost 4 days from work

Total Expenses - $ 100.00 Phone Calls
                     $ 81.18 Private Mechanic
                     $ 207.34 Car Rentals (7 days out of 43)
                     $ 36.59 Postal Fees
                     $ 425.11

Grand Total:

12,792.59
$ ~~12,681.25~~ Purchase Price of Car
$ 297.69 Alarm System
$ 425.11 Expenses to date
~~$ 13,404.05~~
$ 13,515.39

- **Returned** the vehicle to the dealership 7 times for the same complaint - 9 times total

- **Lost** the use of the vehicle for 43 days.

END RESULT:

- **Engine** still misses at idle and now bucks while accelerating.
- **Engine** spits and stalls out on cold starts.
- **Engine** consumes 1/2 gallon of coolant per week.
- **Engine** block still has to be replaced which will take at least 10 days.
  75% disassembly of vehicle.

PURCHASER'S NAME _ANDREW A. FAGLIO_   DATE _4/12/54_

PURCHASER'S ADDRESS _   ZIP CODE _11003_

RESIDENCE PHONE   BUSINESS PHONE   SALESMAN _Bill_

DRIVERS LICENSE #   DATE OF BIRTH   STOCK NO.

INSURANCE CO. AND POLICY #

PLEASE ENTER MY ORDER FOR ONE ☑ _1984_ _Pontiac_   SERIAL NO.

MODEL _Fiero SE_ BODY TYPE _2DR_ BODY COLOR _BLACK_ TOP COLOR   INTERIOR _GRAY_

WARRANTIES ON THIS VEHICLE ARE THE MANUFACTURER'S. THE SELLER HEREBY EXPRESSLY DISCLAIMS ALL WARRANTIES EITHER EXPRESSED OR IMPLIED, INCLUDING ANY IMPLIED WARRANTY OF MERCHANTABILITY OR FITNESS FOR A PARTICULAR PURPOSE AND NEITHER ASSUMES NOR AUTHORIZES ANY OTHER PERSON TO ASSUME FOR IT ANY LIABILITY IN CONNECTION WITH THE SALE OF THE VEHICLE. THIS DISCLAIMER BY THE SELLER IN NO WAY AFFECTS

UPON NOTIFICATION THAT
**VEHICLE IS READY - CUSTOMER
HAS 72 HOURS TO TAKE DELIVERY**

THE PURCHASER WARRANTS THAT ANY USED VEHICLE TRADED HEREIN DOES NOT HAVE A CRACKED ENGINE BLOCK OR CHASSIS AND THAT THE SAME HAS NOT BEEN WELDED AND THAT THE POWER TRAIN IS IN OPERATING CONDITION.

IF YOU AGREE TO ASSIST ME IN OBTAINING FINANCING FOR ANY PART OF THE PURCHASE PRICE, THIS ORDER SHALL NOT BE BINDING UPON YOU OR ME UNTIL ALL OF THE CREDIT TERMS ARE PRESENTED TO ME IN ACCORDANCE WITH REGULATION "Z" (TRUTH-IN-LENDING) AND ARE ACCEPTED BY ME. IF I DO NOT ACCEPT THE CREDIT TERMS WHEN PRESENTED, I MAY CANCEL THIS ORDER AND MY DEPOSIT WILL BE REFUNDED.

IF THIS ORDER IS CANCELLED BY THE BUYER WITHOUT DEALER'S CONSENT, BUYER SHALL BE LIABLE TO DEALER FOR ANY DAMAGE THAT DEALER MAY SUSTAIN THEREFROM.

FILL OUT THIS SECTION IF USED CAR IS TRADED IN

MAKE _   YEAR

BODY TYPE _   MILEAGE

ENGINE SERIAL NO.

LIC. PLATE NO.

USED CAR ALLOWANCE $

ENGINE		POWER DOOR LOCKS
TRANS _4 spd_	☑	REAR DEFOGGER _Std._ ☑
AIR COND	☑	MIRROR _Std_ ☑
TINTED GLASS	☑	WHITE WALL TIRES ☐
POWER STEERING	☐	WHEEL COVERS _Alloy_ ☑
POWER BRAKES	☑	Visor Vanity
POWER WINDOWS	☑	Stereo Cassette
ADDITIONAL EQUIPMENT		Tilt Wheel
Sunroof		
Wheel Locks.		Cruise
Mats		Door Ack B.
Leather Wrap Wheel		Top Shelf

DLR. INST. OPTIONS Not under GM warranty

LIEN HOLDER -

**ALL BALANCES MUST BE PAID IN CASH.
CASHIERS OR CERTIFIED CHECK ONLY.**

FOR OUR MUTUAL PROTECTION CASHIERS OR CERTIFIED CHECK PREFERRED.
Purchaser agrees that this Order includes all of the terms and conditions on both the face and reverse side hereof and that this Order is not subject to cancellation. This Order cancels and supersedes any prior agreement and as of the date hereof comprises the entire agreement relating to the subject matters covered hereby, and that **THIS ORDER SHALL NOT BECOME BINDING UNTIL ACCEPTED BY DEALER OR HIS AUTHORIZED REPRESENTATIVE.** Purchaser by his execution of this Order acknowledges that he has read its terms and conditions and has received a copy of this Order. Buyer certifies he is of legal age to execute binding contract.

Andrew A. Faglio   _4/12/54_
PURCHASER'S SIGNATURE   DATE

SALESMAN _W. Pert_   SALES MANAGER

TOTAL VEHICLE PRICE	$11,700	—
SALES TAX	965	25
N Y S INSPECTION	6	
"DEALER'S FEE FOR OBTAINING REGISTRATION AND OR CERTIFICATE OF TITLE. (FEE MAY NOT EXCEED TEN DOLLARS)"	10	00
FUEL CHARGE		
TOTAL CASH DELIVERED PRICE	12,681	25
DEPOSIT ☐CASH ☒CHECK	300	—
USED CAR ALLOWANCE		
TOTAL CREDITS		
CASH ON DELIVERY	$12,381	25

SPECIAL ORDERS CAN NOT BE CANCELLED.

viii

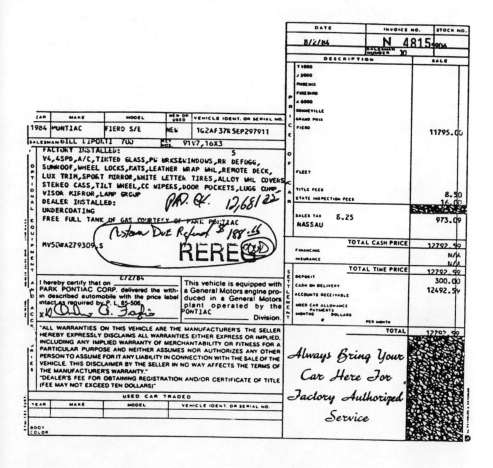

DATE	INVOICE NO.	STOCK NO.
8/2/84	N 4815	904

SALESMAN NUMBER XO

DESCRIPTION	SALE
T 1000	
J 2000	
PHOENIX	
FIREBIRD	
A 6000	
BONNEVILLE	
GRAND PRIX	
FIERO	11795.00
FLEET	
TITLE FEES	8.50
STATE INSPECTION FEES	16.00
SALES TAX 8.25 NASSAU	973.09
TOTAL CASH PRICE	12792.59
FINANCING	N/A
INSURANCE	N/A
TOTAL TIME PRICE	12792.59
DEPOSIT	300.00
CASH ON DELIVERY	12492.59
ACCOUNTS RECEIVABLE	
USED CAR ALLOWANCE	
MONTHS PAYMENTS DOLLARS	
PER MONTH	
TOTAL	12792.59

CAR	MAKE	MODEL	NEW OR USED	VEHICLE IDENT. OR SERIAL NO.
1984	PONTIAC	FIERO S/E	NEW	1G2AF37R5EP297911

SALESMAN BILL LIPORTI 700 KEY NOS. 91V7, 16X3

FACTORY INSTALLED: 5
V4, 4SPD, A/C, TINTED GLASS, PW BRKS&WINDOWS, RR DEFOGG,
SUNROOF, WHEEL LOCKS, RATS, LEATHER WRAP WHL, REMOTE DECK,
LUX TRIM, SPORT MIRROR, WHITE LETTER TIRES, ALLOY WHL COVERS,
STEREO CASS, TILT WHEEL, CC WIPERS, DOOR POCKETS, LUGG COMP,
VISOR MIRROR, LAMP GROUP
DEALER INSTALLED: PAD. OK. 12/68/22
UNDERCOATING
FREE FULL TANK OF GAS COURTESY OF PARK PONTIAC

Aston Due Refund $188.66
RERE OK

MV50 #A279309.S

I hereby certify that on 8/2/84
PARK PONTIAC CORP. delivered the within described automobile with the price label
intact as required by P. L. 85-506.
X

This vehicle is equipped with
a General Motors engine produced in a General Motors
plant operated by the
PONTIAC
_____ Division.

"ALL WARRANTIES ON THIS VEHICLE ARE THE MANUFACTURER'S THE SELLER
HEREBY EXPRESSLY DISCLAIMS ALL WARRANTIES EITHER EXPRESS OR IMPLIED,
INCLUDING ANY IMPLIED WARRANTY OF MERCHANTABILITY OR FITNESS FOR A
PARTICULAR PURPOSE AND NEITHER ASSUMES NOR AUTHORIZES ANY OTHER
PERSON TO ASSUME FOR IT ANY LIABILITY IN CONNECTION WITH THE SALE OF THE
VEHICLE. THIS DISCLAIMER BY THE SELLER IN NO WAY AFFECTS THE TERMS OF
THE MANUFACTURER'S WARRANTY."
"DEALER'S FEE FOR OBTAINING REGISTRATION AND/OR CERTIFICATE OF TITLE
(FEE MAY NOT EXCEED TEN DOLLARS)"

USED CAR TRADED			
YEAR	MAKE	MODEL	VEHICLE IDENT. OR SERIAL NO.

BODY COLOR

Always Bring Your
Car Here For
Factory Authorized
Service

SIX PART FOLDER - SECTION V

I used this section of the six part folder to store all of the important information/correspondence that transpired between my lawyer and me during my case. Reproduced for the reader's benefit are copies of the **Summons and Complaint,** the **Interrogatories** (with my written answers), and the **Final Judgment or Release.** A more detailed explanation of these documents can be found in Chapter 6.

SUPREME COURT OF THE STATE OF NEW YORK
COUNTY OF NASSAU
--x

ANDREW FAGLIO,   :

                    Plaintiff,   :   AFFIDAVIT

                                        :

                                        :   Index #88/86

                                        :

                                        :

--x

STATE OF NEW YORK)
) ss :
COUNTY OF NASSAU)

        I, ANDREW FAGLIO, being duly sworn, hereby deposes
and says that:

        1. That on August 1, 1984, I purchased a new
Pontiac Fiero from   the Defendant herein.
The purchase price including finance charges was TWELVE
THOUSAND SEVEN HUNDRED AND NINETY-two ($12,792.59) DOLLARS
AND FIFTY-NINE CENTS. (Exhibit A)

        2. That on September 26, 1984 I returned to the
dealership to have a steering damper replaced. The vehicle
had 3,988 miles on at that time. The Defendants acknowledged
this by virtue of their work order #W5S90. (Exhibit B)

        3. That in the several days preceding February
7, 1985 I noticed a considerable loss of power while operating
the automobile. In addition, it became obvious that the
engine's idle was not smooth and "missed" frequently. I

then brought the car to the Defendant dealership and complained for the first time about the uneven and irregular running of the motor. See work order #7666 (Exhibit C)

4. That on February 11, 1985 I again returned to the Defendant's shop complaining of irregular motor functioning (Exhibit D)

5. That on February 21, 1985, with 9,642 miles on my car I returned to the dealer because the car would barely run. An "injector" was replaced and the vehicle was out of service eleven days. (Exhibit E)

6. That on March 6, 1985, pursuant to work order WO5121 the dealer replaced a defective radiator overflow tank due to an overheated engine. (Exhibit F)

7. On March 25, 1985 the Defendant, after my complaint of bad idling, attempted to reset idle and timing, WO8416.

8. That on April 18, 1985 I registered a complaint with the Better Business Bureau. (Exhibit G)

9. That on April 22, 1985 I took the car to an independent certified mechanic

diagnosed the problem with my car as "worn timing gear due to a defective condition existing in the vehicle." (Exhibit H)

10. That on May 2, 1985, I, at the urging of the Better Business Bureau, brought the vehicle back to

the dealer. The dealer ordered an engine block although it was never installed. Again the engine was checked for problems and none could be found. See W09141 (Exhibit I)

11.   That on June 20, 1985, the vehicle had to be returned to the dealer because the electric motor which operates the fan that cools the engine burned out due to the engine's overheated condition. See W09873 (Exhibit J).

12.   That I have lost the use of this car for a total of forty-three days due to repair, and the car is presently up on blocks at my home since I cannot effectively use the car. I have had to rent alternate means of transportation which has cost me over $250.00. (Exhibit K)

13.   That I have been forced to retain legal counsel in an action which I feel the Defendant could have easily resolved.

14.   That I went to an orbitration meeting with all the evidence. The arbitration ruled that the defect is not that substantial and that   should be allowed to attempt another repair. The dealership wants to replace the lower half of my engine. This job costs approximately $6,351.50. I do not see how any reasonable man can stand in front of people and state that engine replacement is not the result of a substantial defect. My independent mechanic has supplied me with an estimate for the value of the intended repair work. (Exhibits L and M)

15. That I was present when the arbitrator stated he had little or no knowledge of the motor functions of an automobile. My own thorough investigation has revealed that Pontiac has acknowledged a problem in their Fiero models and has undertaken steps to correct the existing defects when complained of. The problem in my case is that not only did   not recognize the defect early enough, they also went about diagnosing my problem in derogation with accepted Factory Manual Procedures. (Exhibit N) As a result of the Defendant's incompetence, my situation worsened daily.

16. A problem discussed in a recent article in Popular Mechanics has been brought to my attention. The article or answer was written by a noted automotive repair and diagnostician expert. I know becuase as an engineer I read his articles with regularity. In Mr. Schultz' August 1985 column he writes that:

> "The story is that many 1984
> Fiero's that were operated in cold
> Weather have experienced cracked blocks
> at the engine parting line. The parting
> line is where the upper and lower parts
> of the block are cast together".

The person who wrote in to Mr. Schultz had similar symptoms as my Pontiac did when I first perceived the irregular running of the motor vehicle.

If coolant is allowed to mix with the oil in the engine's crank case, over a short period of time oil viscosity will prematurely break down and the result will be a weakened

engine due to excessive friction brought on by the breakdown
of the oil's viscosity. (Exhibit O- Popular Mechanics,
8/85, Mort Schultz)

As it applies to my situation Pontiac's approval
to replace the lower half of my engine is "too little too
late". The consequential damages have already occurred.

17. Notwithstanding the fact that the lower half
of the engine is replaced, I certainly did not bargain
for a vehicle with these problems.

18. I feel that to allow the Defendant to proceed
to a trial I cannot afford would be to allow them to emasculate
the statute which specifically addresses this situation.
I believe that the Legislature had my situation in mind
when it decided to limit the number of times a person like
me has to put up with a bandaid repair program.

_____
ANDREW FAGLIO

SWORN to before me this
      day of February 1986.

_____
          Notary Public

```
SUPREME COURT OF THE STATE OF NEW YORK
COUNTY OF NASSAU
- - - - - - - - - - - - - - - - - - -X
ANDREW FAGLIO,                              :

                    Plaintiff,
                                            :     VERIFIED COMPLAINT
        -against                            :

                                            :

        Defendants.     :
- - - - - - - - - - - - - - - - - - -X
```

        Plaintiff, by his attorney, GEORGE J. HAGGERTY,
ESQ., complaining of the Defendant, alleges as follows:

        1. At all times hereinafter mentioned Plaintiff
was and is a resident of
                        State of New York.

        2. That upon information and belief, the Defendant
                was and is a domestic corporation with
its principal place of business located at

                                            and State
of New York.

        3. That upon information and belief the Defendant,
                        was and is a foreign
corporation authorized and doing business in the State of
New York.

        4. That on August 2, 1984 the Defendants sold
the Plaintiff a 1984 POntiac Fiero, Vehicle Identification
Number 1G2AF37R5EP297911, for the sum of ELEVEN THOUSAND

SEVEN HUNDRED AND NINETY-FIVE ($11,795.00) DOLLARS, excluding tax and financing charges.

5. That the aforementioned vehicle was materially defective in numerous respects, including but not limited to a cracked and defective engine.

6. That the aforementioned defects required in excess of eleven (11) service visits to the Defendants' premises and at least seven (7) of said visits were due to the same defect, namely a cracked and defective engine.

7. That due to the aforementioned service visits the Plaintiff was deprived of the use of the subject automobile for more than forty-five (45) days in a six-month period.

8. Plaintiff has attempted arbitration and does not accept the resolution as decided by a party who admitted no knowledge whatsoever of the function of an automobile.

9. That despite actual and constructive notice of the defective condition of the enginie of the Plintiff's vehicle and of the engines of most cars of that model the Defendancs' service agents negligently and improperly serviced the Plaintiff's automobile.

10. That prompt correction of stated defect could have prevented further engine wear due to coolant seepage.

11. That the Defendants' mechanics should have reasonably foreseen the damages which would result from both coolant seepage and the stated engine defect.

12.   That Defendants' negligence in not foreseeing stated subsequent damage proximately caused the present defective state of the entire engine.

13.   That due to the negligent actions of the Defendants and their agents, the Plaintiff's vehicle has sustained serious and substantial damage to the entire "power train" assembly and that said damage has substantially impaired the value and performance of said vehicle.

14.   That the aforesaid damage includes but is not limited to coolant seepage, viscosity breakdown and premature engine wear.

15.   That the Plaintiff has provided the Defendants with more than eleven (11) opportunities to cure and repair the defective condition described herein and that the Defendants have failed, refused and been unable to do so.

16.   That the Plaintiff has been damaged by being unable to use the vehicle in question and having to rent substitute transportation.

17.   That the Plainitiff is no longer of the opinion that the Defendants can cure stated engine defects in this particular vehicle due to the negligent past performance of Defendants' mechanics which contributed to the defective engine conditions.

18.   That the Defendant has been damaged in that the aforesaid defects detract greatly from the value of the vehicle in question.

19. That the Plaintiff's damages are in excess of TEN THOUSAND ($10,000.00) DOLLARS.

WHEREFORE, the Plaintiff requests monetary compensation pursuant to NYS GBL Section 198b. Moreover, Plaintiff asks the Court to award damages which take into consideration any and all contract and warranty remedies available at law or equity as well as those remedies which deal with the negligent maintenance of the Plaintiff's automobile. Lastly, Plaintiff respectfully requests the Court to grant attorneys' fees from the Defendants both pursuant to GBL Section 198b and the nature of this consumer action.

Dated:
      September 26, 1985.

                Yours, etc.,

SUPREME COURT OF THE STATE OF NEW YORK
COUNTY OF NASSAU
---x
ANDREW FAGLIO,

                Plaintiff,   :

      -against-   :   INTERROGATORIES

                           :

                Defendants.   :
---x

    Defendant,   (hereinafter re-
ferred to as "General Motors"), hereby requests that the plaintiff,
ANDREW FAGLIO   , answer the interrogatories hereinafter set
forth in accordance with Article 31 of the Civil Practice Law and
Rules:

<u>INSTRUCTIONS</u>

(a) CPLR 3134(a) requires all answers to be
made in writing under oath and that each
answer shall be preceded by the question to
which it responds.

(b) If any question cannot be answered fully,
so state and explain. Furnish all information
available to the Plaintiff(s). If it is believed
that any information requested is in the
possession of another, so state and give appropriate
names and addresses.

(c) As used herein, the terms, "writing", "writings",
"document", "documents", and "documentation" include,
but are not limited to, books, records, statements,
letters, telegrams, notes, memoranda, minutes,
reports, summaries, forecasts, appraisals, surveys,
opinions, calculations, diaries, worksheets, drafts,
photographs, photocopies, drawings, originals and
copies, and other tangible things, whether typed
or handwritten or on tape, photo or other recording,
from whatever source.

1. Set forth the make, model, model year and vehicle
identification number of the motor vehicle, which is the subject
matter of this action.

2. Set forth the name and address of the purchaser and
registered owner of the motor vehicle.

3. ✓ Was the vehicle purchased from a dealer's inventory or was it specially ordered?   Furnish a complete and legible copy of the purchase order or agreement.

4. ✓ State the date the vehicle was purchased and furnish a complete and legible copy of the Bill of Sale, financing agreement (if any) and any other proofs of purchase.

5. ✓ Set forth the name and address of the person or company from whom plaintiff purchased the motor vehicle.

6. ✓ List and furnish complete, legible copies of all written warranties, service agreements and mechanical breakdown insurance received or purchased allegedly covering the motor vehicle which is the subject matter of this action.

7. ✓ If plaintiff claims an additional oral warranty, then set forth as precisely as possible the substance of such warranty, the date and place made and the name and title of the person, who allegedly made such warranty.

8. ✓ For each claimed "defect" which the plaintiff alleges was not repaired or corrected properly by the defendants (or persons or companies acting on their behalf) set forth the following information:

> (a) a general description of the problem as observed or experienced by the driver.
>
> (b) the exact part or parts or subassemblies which are claimed to have been defective,.describing the defect.
>
> (c) the specific dates and odometer readings when the identified problem was brought to the attention of one of the defendants, (or persons or companies acting on their behalf), identifying the place, the defendant and the particular persons to whom such communications were made, and give complete details of each such communication including statements and responses by all parties involved.
>
> (d) state whether the defect was corrected or repaired, and if so, identify the person or company who effected such repair.

Separately, for each problem alleged to be caused by a defect, answer all the above four parts of this question. We are seeking a problem by problem analysis, not lists. Set forth your answers in prose; do not answer by reference to documents.

(e) identify by problem described and furnish copies of all bills, repair orders, correspondence and other records and documents pertaining to the problem and to the answers given.

9. For the $10,000.00 damages claimed in complaint paragraph "19",
describe each and every element or item of the alleged damages and the dollar amount thereof.

(a) separately, for each element or item of damage so identified, describe the method used to determine such damages showing calculation. (Do not answer by

(b) making specific reference to the applicable elements or items of damages so identified or described, furnish copies of all bills, books, records and other writings utilized by plaintiff to establish the dollar amount of such alleged element or item of damage.

10. State whether or not the vehicle is still owned by the plaintiff. If still owned, set forth the present odometer reading. If not owned, give full particulars concerning its disposition, including, but not limited to, purchasers, price, date and odometer reading. Furnish copies of all writings pertaining to such disposition.

11. Other than the damages set forth in answer to interrogatory "9" above and attorneys' fees,
will plaintiff be claiming any other damages of any kind?

If the answer is yes, then describe each and every element or item of such other damages and the dollar amounts thereof, and

(a) separately, for each element or item of damage
so identified, describe the method used to determine
such damages showing calculation. (Do not answer
by referring to documents or attachments.)

(b) making specific reference to the applicable
elements or items of damages so identified or described,
furnish copies of all bills, books, records and other
writings utilized by plaintiff to establish the
dollar amount or such alleged element or item of
damage.

12. If the complaint alleges that plaintiff attempted
to effect revocation of sale of the subject motor vehicle, set
forth in detail every action taken by plaintiff in an attempt to
effect revocation with dates, odometer readings and persons
involved, indicating both oral and written communications,
and furnish legible copies of all pertinent writings.

13. Give full particulars of the understanding between
the plaintiff and its attorney regarding the payment of attorneys'
fees. Identify and furnish copies of any and all relevant
writings.

14. Separately for each of the "defects" identified in
answer to Interrogatory "8" above; set forth the dates the vehicle
was in an authorized dealership for repairs pertaining to the
identified "defect".

PLEASE TAKE NOTICE that a copy of answers to these
interrogatories must be served upon the undersigned within fifteen
days after the service of these interrogatories.

George J. Haggerty, Esq.

Dear George,

Enclosed is all the information required to answer the interrogatorites. Contact me if you have any questions or need additional information.

Sincerely,

Andrew A. Faglio

AAF/bg
Enclosures

(1) Pontiac, Fiero SE, 1984, 1G2AF37RSEP297911

(2) Purchaser and Registered Owner:

George, I do not know which address you wanted to use. The first
address is the one that appears on the order and bill of sale.

(3) o Vehicle was ordered new from the factory.

     o Copy of order form attached.

(4) o Vehicle was purchased August 2, 1984.

     o Copy of purchase attached.

(5)

(6) George - You have my warranty book.

(7) No oral warranties were made to me. Prior to purchase, however, the
     salesman stated "Don't worry about buying a first year car because the
     engine and drive train are tried and true and have been in numerous GM
     cars since 1980."

(8)

Date	Work Order Number	Odometer Mileage	Narrative	Number of Days
9/26/84	W5890	3,988	Defective steering damper replaced.	1
2/7/85	W7666	8,972	1st complaint that engine was missing at idle. Dealer replaced one ignition wire (#4 plug wire).	1
2/11/85	W7690	9,015	2nd complaint that engine was missing at idle. Dealer replaced #1,2,3 ignition wires. Poor workmanship wires poorly routed over intake manifold, all wire looms broken. Timing set to TDC instead of 8° BTC; idle set to 1,150 RPMs instead of 950. (Band-aid fix).	1
2/21/85	W08051	9,642	3rd complaint that engine was missing at idle. Dealer installed an injector. Vehicle out of service for 11 days waiting for parts (2/22/85 thru 3/4/85).	11

Date	Work Order Number	Odometer Mileage	Narrative	Number of Days
3/25/85	W08416	10,600	4th complaint that engine was missing at idle. Dealer told me that the engine was not missing. The idle was set at 1,100 RPMs instead of 950; timing set to 12° BTC instead of 8° BTC. (Band-aid fix #2). When I picked up the vehicle, it was still missing and demonstrated said condition to the service manager	1
3/06/85	W08121	9,824	Dealer replaced defective radiator overflow tank.	1
4/18/85	BBB Code 40121	10,800	Complaint registered with the Better Business Bureau so that arbitration date could be set.	
4/19/85			Retained legal counsel.	
4/22/85	44611	11,000	Took vehicle to an independent certified mechanic.	1
4/26/85	W09059	12,223	5th complaint of engine missing. Vehicle returned to dealer for diagnosis by District Service Manager. Result - Front portion of engine has to be disassembled at a future date so that problem can be assessed further.	1
4/30/85			Registered formal complaint letters sent	
5/2/85	W09141	12,310	6th complaint of engine missing. Problem diagnosed as porous engine block. The engine coolant is mixing with the engine oil. Water in the oil. Dealer offered to replace the block. I refused on the grounds that the car is a lemon and that the dealer is	13

Date	Work Order Number	Odometer Mileage	Narrative	Number of Days
			not capable of doing an adequate job. This is witnessed by the fact that previous visits to the dealer resulted in shoddy workmanship and band-aid fixes.	
6/20/85	W09873	12,400	Electric Radiator cooling fan motor "shorted out" resulting in the engine overheating and the melting of the fan blade assembly.	12

7th complaint of engine missing. Vehicle out of service 6/20/85 thru 7/2/85. I rented two Hertz cars for 7 out of the 12 days.

Hertz Bill #63786979-4 $105.80

#63787050-5 $101.54

$207.34

- Returned the vehicle to the dealership 7 times for the same complaint -10 times total.
- Lost the use of the vehicle for 43 days.

END RESULT:

- Engine still misses at idle and now bucks while accelerating.
- Engine spits and stalls out on cold starts.
- Engine consumes 1/2 gallon of coolant per week.
- Engine block still has to be replaced which will take at least 10 days. 75% disassembly of vehicle.

(9) Ask George.

(10) o Vehicle is still owned by plaintiff and has been taken off the road since August 16, 1985.

o Odometer Reading - 12,763 miles.

(11)   Expenses to date - George are there any additional fees?

         $100.00 Phone Calls $80.00 Service of Documents
          81.18 Private Mechanic   25.00 Process of Papers to G.M.
         207.34 Car Rentals   25.00 Consultation Fee
          36.59 Postal Fees   400.00 Interrogatory Fee ?

       2,700.00 Purchase of used interim vehicle (1979 Chevy Caprice)
         300.00 Cost increase of insuring two vehicles
      12,792.89 Purchase Price of 1984 Pontiac Fiero SE
         297.69 Alarm System

(12) George's Responsibility - Also the whole BBB arbitration proceedings.
(13)   "   "   - What about my registered letters to GM people?

(14) Vehicle was taken to the authorized dealership -   for
     all repairs pertaining to all the defects denoted in Section 8.

SUPREME COURT OF THE STATE OF NEW YORK
COUNTY OF NASSAU
---X

                    Plaintiff,

          -against-   RELEASE

                                                Index Number
                                                88/1986
                    Defendants.
---X

          TO ALL WHOM THESE PRESENTS SHALL COME OR MAY
CONCERN, THAT
                    ANDREW FAGLIO

as Releasor, in consideration of the sum of
THIRTEEN THOUSAND FIVE HUNDRED DOLLARS AND NO CENTS
                         $13.500.00
received from

as Releasees, receipt whereof is hereby acknowledged,
releases and discharges

the heirs, executors, administrators, successors, and
assigns from all actions, suits, debts, dues, sums of
money, accounts reckoning, bonds, bills, specialties,
covenants, contracts, controversies, agreemtns, promises,
variances, trespasses, damages, judgments and claims whatsoever,
in law, admiralty or equity, which against the Releasees,
the Releasors, Releasor's heirs, executors, administrators,
successors and assigns ever had, now have or hereafter
can, shall or may, have for, upon, or by reason of any
matter, cause or thing whatsoever from the beginning of
the world to the day of the date of the RELEASE. This
RELEASE shall not be construed to imply any liability
or complicity on the part of the Releases in any tortious
act by whomever committed.

Whenever the text hereof requires, the use of singular
number shall include the appropriate plural number as
the text of the within instrument may require.

This RELEASE may not be changed orally.

          IN WITNESS WHEREOF, the Releasors have hereunto
set Releasors' hand and seal on the day of *22nd of December*
1986

                              Andrew Faglio (L.S.)
                              JANICE Y. MURPHY
IN THE PRESENCE OF   Notary Public, State of New York
                                   No. 52-4601514
                              Qualified in Suffolk County

SUPREME COURT OF THE STATE OF NEW YORK
COUNTY OF NASSAU

--X

ANDREW FAGLIO,

                    Plaintiff,

                                        STIPULATION OF
                                        DISCONTINUANCE

                                        Index Number 88/1986

--X

       IT IS HEREBY STIPULATED AND AGREED by and between
GEORGE J. HAGGERTY ESQ., attorney for Plaintiff, and

       Defendants, that the above captioned action is
hereby discontinued.

Dated: Garden City, New York
        December 11, 1986

                                _____
                                GEORGE J HAGGERTY, ESQ.
                                Attorney for Plaintiff

                                _____
                                PARK PONTIAC CORP. and
                                GENERAL MOTORS CORP. -
                                PARK PONTIAC DIVISION
                                Defendants

APPENDIX B

New York State New Vehicle Lemon Law Questions and Answers

Appendix B is taken from "New York's New Car Lemon Law: A Guide for Consumers." which is produced by the New York State Department of Law Office of Public Information.

STATE OF NEW YORK
DEPARTMENT OF LAW
120 BROADWAY
NEW YORK, NY 10271

ROBERT ABRAMS
Attorney General

Dear New Yorker:

New cars are getting more and more expensive. For their money, buyers are entitled to receive a car that meets reasonable standards of quality, reliability and performance, and most new cars do. However, each year my office receives many complaints from consumers who purchase new cars which turn out to be "lemons". Purchasers of defective cars should be able to get them repaired or replaced promptly.

Until 1987, consumers with new cars plagued with serious defects faced an almost insurmountable burden in winning lemon law redress. They were required either to commence a lawsuit or to seek redress through the manufacturer's own arbitration programs. Realistically, neither option adequately served consumers.

Consequently, an alternative neutral dispute resolution was imperative to permit consumers to exercise effectively their lemon law rights and so the Legislature established the New York Lemon Law Arbitration Program.

This program provides New York consumers with an independent, inexpensive, speedy and effective forum to present and resolve lemon law grievances. Since its inception in 1987, the program has already proven itself to be the largest and most successful lemon law arbitration program in the nation. Thousands of consumers have participated in it and recoveries have totaled in excess of $60 million.

This booklet was prepared by my staff to help you understand the New Car Lemon Law and the New York State Arbitration Program. New Yorkers who need additional asistance or information about new car problems should contact the Attorney General's office nearest them.

Sincerely,

ROBERT ABRAMS
Attorney General

i

New Car Lemon Law
Questions and Answers

**WHAT IS THE PURPOSE OF THE
NEW YORK NEW CAR LEMON LAW?**
The New Car Lemon Law (General Business Law § 198-a) provides a legal remedy for consumers who are buyers or lessees of new cars and certain used cars (see next question) that turn out to be lemons. If the car does not conform to the terms of the written warranty and the manufacturer or its authorized dealer is unable to repair the car after a reasonable number of attempts during the first 18,000 miles or two years, whichever comes first, the consumer can choose a full refund or a comparable replacement car. A copy of the law may be found in the back of this booklet.

**WHICH CARS ARE COVERED
BY THE LEMON LAW?**
The law covers both new and used cars, including "demos", which satisfy the following four conditions:

1. The car was covered by the manufacturer's new car warranty at the time of original delivery; and
2. The car was purchased, leased or transferred within the earlier of the first 18,000 miles or two years from the date of original delivery; and
3. The car either: (a) was purchased, leased or transferred in New York, or (b) is presently registered in New York; and
4. The car is primarily used for personal purposes.

Some examples of cars that are covered by the new car lemon law are:
* a new car purchased from a New York dealer and registered in New York;
* a new car leased from a New Jersey dealer and registered in New York;
* a demonstrator car with 10,000 miles purchased from a New York dealer and registered in New Jersey;
* a used car with 13,000 miles purchased from a Connecticut dealer and registered in New York;
* a used car with 11,000 miles received as a gift from a friend and registered in New York.

WHAT DOES THE PHRASE "PRIMARILY USED FOR PERSONAL PURPOSES" MEAN?

A car is primarily used for personal purposes when its principal use is for personal, family or household purposes. Such purposes include, for example, using the car for household errands or to drive to and from work. A car may be used for mixed personal and business use provided that the personal use is predominant. In one recent lemon law case, the court ruled that if the car is used 85% of the time for personal use and only 15% of the time for business use, it is covered.

ARE MOTOR HOMES COVERED?

Motor homes are also covered under the law, except as to defects in systems, fixtures, appliances or other parts that are residential in character. However, motor home complaints are subject to special notification requirements. (See page 5.)

ARE MOTORCYCLES AND OFF-ROAD VEHICLES COVERED?

Motorcycles and off-road vehicles are not covered by the law.

ARE ALL LEASED CARS COVERED?

The law covers only those leased cars where the lessee is responsible for repairs of the car.

ARE CARS OWNED BY BUSINESSES COVERED?

The question of whether cars owned by corporations or businesses, although used primarily for personal purposes may qualify for lemon law relief, has not been finally resolved. Lower courts have taken opposing views on this issue.

WHAT IS THE MANUFACTURER'S DUTY TO REPAIR?

With respect to those covered cars sold and registered in New York, the law imposes a duty upon the manufacturer to repair, free of charge and without any deductible, any defect covered by warranty, if the consumer notifies the manufacturer or its authorized dealer of such defect within the first 18,000 miles of operation or two years from the original delivery date, whichever comes first. Once timely notice of the defect is given, the manufacturer may not charge for the repairs, regardless of when the repairs are performed. Any consumer who has been charged for such repairs or a deductible during such period should contact the Attorney General's office.

WHAT SHOULD CONSUMERS DO
IF THEY BECOME AWARE OF A
PROBLEM WITH THEIR CAR?

The consumer should immediately report any defect or "condition" either directly to the manufacturer or to its authorized dealer. A "condition" is a general problem, such as a difficulty in starting, repeated stalling, or a malfunctioning transmission, that can result from a defect of one or more parts. If the consumer reports the problem to the dealer, the law requires the dealer to forward written notice to the manufacturer within seven days. Under the law, notice to the dealer is considered notice to the manufacturer. Unless otherwise advised by their lawyer, consumers should continue to make their monthly payments if the car is financed or leased. Failure to do so may result in a repossession which may, adversely affect a consumer's lemon law rights.

WHAT SHOULD A CONSUMER DO IF
THE DEALER REFUSES TO MAKE REPAIRS?

If the dealer refuses to make repairs within seven days of receiving notice from the consumer, the consumer should immediately notify the manufacturer in writing, by certified mail, return receipt requested, of the car's problem and that the dealer has refused to make repairs. A sample notice to the manufacturer may be found on page 19.

WHAT MUST THE MANUFACTURER DO
UPON RECEIPT OF THE CONSUMER'S NOTICE
OF THE DEALER'S REFUSAL TO MAKE REPAIRS?

The manufacturer or its authorized dealer must commence repairs within 20 days from receipt of the consumer's notice of the dealer's refusal to make repairs.

WHAT ARE A CONSUMER'S RIGHTS
IF THE MANUFACTURER DOES NOT
MEET ITS DUTY TO REPAIR?

If the problem is not repaired after a reasonable number of attempts, or the manufacturer or the dealer refuses to commence repairs within 20 days from the manufacturer's receipt of the "refusal to repair" notice from the consumer, and if the problem substantially impairs the value of the car to the consumer, the manufacturer, at the consumer's option, must either refund the full purchase or lease price, or offer a comparable replacement car.

DOES THE LAW SPECIFY THE NUMBER
OF REQUIRED REPAIR ATTEMPTS?

It is presumed that there have been a reasonable number of attempts to repair a problem if, during the first 18,000 miles of operation or two years from the original delivery date, whichever comes first, either: (1) the same problem has been subject to repair four or more times and the problem continues to exist; or (2) the car is out of service by reason of repair of one or more problems for a cumulative total of 30 or more calendar days and the problem continues to exist.

WHAT SPECIAL NOTIFICATION REQUIREMENTS EXIST FOR MOTOR HOME OWNERS?

The law imposes special notification requirements for motor homes which are designed to afford motor home manufacturers one final chance to repair the defect before consumers can take advantage of the remedies offered by the lemon law. If the motor home was subject to three repair attempts or was out of service by reason of repair for 21 days, whichever occurs first, the consumer must report such fact to the manufacturer or its authorized dealer by certified mail, return receipt requested, before seeking arbitration or commencing a lawsuit under the lemon law.

MUST A MOTOR HOME MANUFACTURER GIVE CONSUMERS PRIOR WRITTEN NOTICE OF THESE SPECIAL REQUIREMENTS?

The special notification requirements are only applicable if the manufacturer or its authorized dealer has provided the consumer with a written copy of these requirements. Receipt of the notice must be acknowledged by the consumer in writing.

WHAT IF A CONSUMER FAILS TO COMPLY WITH THESE SPECIAL REQUIREMENTS FOR MOTOR HOMES?

Where a consumer fails to comply with the special notification requirements, additional repair attempts or days out of service will not be taken into account in determining the consumer's right to relief. However, additional repair attempts or down time will be considered if they occur after the consumer has complied with the notification requirements.

WHAT CONSTITUTES A SUBSTANTIAL IMPAIRMENT OF VALUE?

It will depend on the facts in each case. In general, the consumer's complaint must be about a serious problem. For example, a defect in the engine which makes the car inoperable is clearly substantial. Some courts have found that the cumulative effect of numerous lesser defects can add up to substantial impairment of value.

ARE THERE ANY EXCEPTIONS
TO THE MANUFACTURER'S DUTY
TO REFUND OR REPLACE?

The manufacturer does not have a duty to make a refund or provide a replacement car if: (1) the problem does not substantially impair the value of the car to the consumer, or (2) the problem is a result of abuse, neglect or unauthorized alteration of the car.

HOW CAN CONSUMERS PROVE
THEY OWN A LEMON?

The consumer must be able to document repeated repair attempts. Therefore, it is very important to keep careful records of all complaints and copies of all work orders, repair bills and correspondence. A dealer is required by Department of Motor Vehicles (DMV) regulations to provide a legible and accurate written work order, upon the request of a consumer, each time any repair work is performed on a car, including warranty work. Consumers may contact the DMV at 1-800-342-3823 if they have a problem obtaining their repair orders.

WHAT SHOULD BE INCLUDED IN
THE CONSUMER'S REFUND?

The refund should include the price of the car (cash plus trade-in allowance), including all options, plus title and registration fees and any other governmental charges, less any lawful deductions.

WHAT ARE THE "LAWFUL DEDUCTIONS"?

The manufacturer may deduct a reasonable amount for mileage in excess of the first 12,000 miles. No deductions may be made for the first 12,000 miles of use. The law states that such deduction shall be calculated by taking the mileage in excess of 12,000 miles times the purchase (or lease) price, divided by 100,000. For example, if a defective car has 15,000 miles on its odometer and cost $10,000, the deduction for use would be $300 (3,000 multiplied by $10,000 divided by 100,000). In addition, a reasonable deduction may be taken for any damage not due to normal wear.

IS THE REFUND AMOUNT
DIFFERENT IF THE PURCHASE
WAS FINANCED?

The refund by the manufacturer is the same whether the car was financed or not. However, when the car is financed, instead of the entire refund going to the consumer, the refund must be divided between the consumer and the lender (the bank or finance company). Generally, the lender will calculate how much is still owed by the consumer and apply the refund to that amount. The balance of the refund will go to the consumer.

IF THE CAR WAS LEASED, HOW
IS THE REFUND CALCULATED?

When the car is leased, the refund due from the manufacturer is divided between the consumer/lessee and the leasing company (the company to which the consumer makes lease payments) according to a formula provided by the law. The lease price to be refunded to the consumer/lessee is the total of the lessee's down payment (including any trade-in allowance) plus the total of monthly lease payments, minus interest charges and any other service fees. For example, suppose that a consumer leases a new car under a three-year lease, makes a $1,500 down payment, and pays a monthly lease payment of $300. Of the $300 monthly payment, an average of $75 is allocated as interest charges. After making twelve monthly payments, the lessee is granted a refund under the lemon law. The refund will be $4,200 calculated as follows:

Deposit	$ 1,500	
+ Monthly Payments. .	+ 3,600	(12x300)
	$ 5,100	
- minus interest	- 900	(12x75)
total refund	$ 4,200	

If the monthly payment includes other service fees, such as insurance or other costs, paid for the benefit of the lessee, such amounts will be deducted from the refund. The leasing company's portion of the refund is the balance of the "lease price", as that term is defined by the law.

IF THE CAR IS LEASED, DOES
A DETERMINATION THAT THE CAR
IS A LEMON TERMINATE THE LEASE?

Once a determination has been made under the lemon law that a car is a lemon, the lease is terminated. As a result, *no* early termination penalties under the lease may be collected.

DOES A SUCCESSFUL CONSUMER
RECOVER SALES TAX?

State and local sales taxes are refunded directly by the New York State Commissioner of Taxation and Finance who will determine the appropriate amount to be refunded under the law. Consumers must complete and submit an "Application for Refund of State and Local Sales Tax" (Form AU-11) to the New York State Department of Taxation and Finance, Central Office Audit Bureau - Sales Tax, State Campus, Albany, N.Y. 12227. (Such form may be obtained through the manufacturer or directly from the Commissioner of Taxation and Finance.) A consumer has three years from the date a refund is received from the manufacturer to apply for the tax refund.

WHAT IS A "COMPARABLE
REPLACEMENT VEHICLE"?
Appellate courts have ruled that the lemon law does not entitle a consumer who elects to receive a "comparable replacement vehicle" instead of a refund, to receive a new vehicle. Rather, the consumer is entitled to receive a car of the same year and model and which has approximately the same mileage as the car being replaced.

HOW CAN A CONSUMER'S RIGHTS
UNDER THE LEMON LAW BE ENFORCED?
A consumer has the choice of either participating in an arbitration program or suing the manufacturer directly in court. If a manufacturer has established an arbitration procedure which complies with federal regulations and the state's lemon law, the manufacturer may refuse to provide a refund until the consumer first participates in such procedure or in the state-run arbitration program. Any action under the lemon law must be commenced within four years of the date of original delivery.

IF THE CONSUMER WINS IN COURT,
CAN ATTORNEY'S FEES ALSO BE RECOVERED?
The law authorizes the court to award reasonable attorney's fees to a successful consumer.

WHAT IS AN ARBITRATION PROCEEDING?
An arbitration proceeding is much less complicated, time consuming and expensive than going to court. The arbitration hearing is informal and strict rules of evidence do not apply. Arbitrators, rather than judges, listen to each side, review the evidence and render a decision.

WHAT ARBITRATION PROGRAMS ARE
AVAILABLE TO CONSUMERS IN NEW YORK?
Consumers may participate in the New York State Lemon Law Arbitration Program ("New York Program"), established by the lemon law. The New York Program is administered by the American Arbitration Association ("AAA") under regulations issued by the Attorney General. (A copy of the regulations may be found in the back of this booklet.) Decisions under the New York Program are binding on both parties. Consumers may also choose to participate in arbitration programs established by auto manufacturers. Decisions under manufacturer programs are not binding on consumers. Consequently, consumers who have gone through the manufacturer's program and are not satisfied may still apply for arbitration under the New York Program. However, any prior arbitration decision may be considered at any subsequent arbitration hearing or court proceeding. The law permits manufacturers to require that consumers first participate in the manufacturer's program, if it complies with federal regulations and the state's lemon law, before suing in court for relief under the lemon law.

HOW DOES A CONSUMER PARTICIPATE
IN THE NEW YORK PROGRAM?
A consumer must first complete a "Request for Arbitration" form, which may be obtained from any of the Attorney General's regional offices. (A list of the Attorney General's regional offices may be found at the end of this booklet). The completed form must be returned to the Attorney General's New Car Lemon Law Arbitration Unit, New York State Department of Law, 120 Broadway, New York, New York 10271.

HOW DOES THE NEW YORK
PROGRAM OPERATE?
The Attorney General's office will review the form to determine whether the consumer's claim is eligible under the lemon law to be heard by an arbitrator. If accepted, the form will be forwarded to the AAA, the Program Administrator, for processing. The AAA will then ask the consumer to pay the required filing fee. Upon receiving the filing fee, the AAA will appoint an arbitrator and schedule a hearing to be held within 35 days. If rejected, the form will be returned to the consumer together with an explanation for the rejection. A complete step-by-step description of the New York Program may be found beginning on page 14 of this booklet.

WHO ARE THE ARBITRATORS?
The arbitrators are volunteers who have been trained in the lemon law and in arbitration procedures by the Attorney General's office and the AAA.

ARE CARS OWNED BY A BUSINESS
ACCEPTED INTO THE NEW YORK PROGRAM?
If a car owned by a business is used primarily for personal, family or household purposes, the fact that the car is owned by a business will not be a basis for the Attorney General's office rejecting a request for arbitration under the New York Program. However, consumers are cautioned that some manufacturers may challenge eligibility for relief under the Lemon Law.

IS A CONSUMER
ENTITLED TO AN ORAL HEARING?
Consumers have an absolute right to an oral hearing. At an oral hearing, both the consumer and the manufacturer's representative will have the opportunity to present their case in person before an arbitrator.

MAY A CONSUMER CHOOSE A HEARING ON DOCUMENTS ONLY?

A consumer may elect to have a hearing on documents only by indicating this preference on the "Request for Arbitration" form . In a "documents only" hearing, both sides must present their positions in writing. If a consumer requests a "documents only" hearing, the manufacturer may object, in which case an oral hearing will be scheduled.

MAY A STENOGRAPHIC RECORD OR TAPE RECORDING BE MADE OF THE HEARING?

Any party to the arbitration may arrange, on its own, for a stenographic record or a tape recording of the hearing at their own expense even if the other party objects. If a stenographer or tape recorder will be used, reasonable prior notice, through the AAA, must be given to the other party.

DOES THE CONSUMER NEED AN ATTORNEY FOR THE ARBITRATION HEARING?

The New York Program is designed to be accessible to consumers without the need for an attorney. However, both the consumer and the manufacturer may use an attorney or any other person to assist them if they so choose.

HOW SHOULD CONSUMERS PREPARE FOR THE HEARING?

Consumers should keep a copy of their "Request for Arbitration" form to use as a guide in preparing for the hearing. The form contains much of the information needed at the hearing. In addition, consumers are advised to:

(a) Gather Documents. Bring to the hearing records of everything pertaining to the purchase and the problem, including a copy of the purchase contract (invoice), all correspondence, work orders, and warranty.
(b) Organize Records. Keep records in chronological order. This will serve as a guide in presenting the history of the problem.
(c) Prepare an Outline. This will help to present and remember relevant information.
(d) Prepare Questions to Ask the Manufacturer's Representative. This will assure that no important question is omitted.
(e) Arrange for Witnesses. The presence of witnesses, especially auto mechanics, or their sworn statements may be helpful to document the problem.

WHAT IF CONSUMERS DO NOT HAVE ALL THE DOCUMENTS?

Upon payment of the filing fee and prior to the hearing, consumers may make a written request to the arbitrator, through the AAA, to direct the manufacturer to provide any necessary documents or other information. Consumers may also request the arbitrator to subpoena documents or witnesses to appear at the hearing. A sample letter requesting documents may be found at page 19 of this booklet.

HOW SHOULD CONSUMERS PRESENT THEIR CASE AT THE HEARING?

At the hearing, consumers should present their case in a clear, organized and concise manner. Consumers are advised to:

(a) State the specific nature of the problem.
(b) State any conversations with the dealer's or manufacturer's representatives.
(c) Describe and document each repair attempt.
(d) Describe and document any new developments which may have occurred since the "Request for Arbitration" form was submitted.
(e) Offer proof of each point, especially those the manufacturer may dispute.
(f) Present any witness that may provide relevant information.
(g) State the relief requested.
(h) At the end of the presentation, briefly summarize the facts discussed.

WHAT HAPPENS IF EITHER PARTY FAILS TO APPEAR AT THE HEARING?

Unless the hearing has been properly rescheduled, if either the manufacturer or the consumer fails to appear at an oral hearing, the arbitrator will nevertheless conduct the hearing and issue a decision based upon the evidence presented and any documents contained in the file.

WHEN CAN A CONSUMER EXPECT A DECISION?

A consumer may expect a decision, generally, within 10 days of the hearing. Sometimes, however, the arbitrator requests that additional documents or information be submitted, in which case the decision may be delayed.

CAN A CONSUMER RECOVER THE FILING FEE?

If the consumer is successful, the arbitrator's decision in favor of the consumer must include the return of the filing fee.

WHEN MUST A MANUFACTURER COMPLY WITH AN ARBITRATOR'S DECISION?

Within thirty days. In most cases, the manufacturer's representative will contact the consumer within this period to arrange for the return of the car in exchange for either a refund or a replacement car. Failure of the manufacturer to comply within this time period entitles the consumer to recover an additional $25 for each business day of noncompliance, up to $500. If the manufacturer does not voluntarily pay any applicable penalty, the consumer may sue to recover this penalty in Small Claims Court. However, this deadline and penalties are not applicable where a consumer requests a car built to order or with options which are not comparable to the car being replaced.

HOW IS A RETURN OF
THE CAR IMPLEMENTED?

The common procedure is to have all the affected parties -- the consumer, the manufacturer's representative, and, if the car is financed or leased, the lender's or the leasing company's representative -- meet at an agreed time and place to execute the necessary papers to exchange the car for a refund or replacement. The consumer may choose to return the car to either the selling dealer or the dealer which attempted to repair the car. No further shipping charges may be imposed on the consumer for the return of the car.

WHAT HAPPENS IF THE MANUFACTURER
DOES NOT COMPLY WITH
THE ARBITRATOR'S AWARD?

If the manufacturer does not comply with the award, a consumer can enforce the arbitrator's decision through the courts by bringing an action to confirm the award. This action must be commenced within one year of receipt of the decision. Consumers should consult a private attorney if they wish to pursue this remedy. If the consumer is successful, the Court will convert the arbitrator's award into a court judgment and may award attorney's fees. The court may also award reasonable attorneys' fees incurred to enforce the collection of the award.

UNDER WHAT CIRCUMSTANCES
CAN AN ARBITRATOR'S DECISION
BE MODIFIED?

The grounds for modification are very limited. Generally, awards may be modified only to correct a miscalculation or a technical mistake in the award. For example, a modification may be requested where the mileage deduction was miscalculated or the filing fee was omitted from the refund.

WHEN MUST A REQUEST FOR
MODIFICATION BE MADE?

Either party may seek a modification by the arbitrator of the award by written application to the AAA within 20 days of receiving the award. The other party will be given the opportunity to object to the modification. The arbitrator must rule on all such requests within 30 days after the request is received. To modify an award after 20 days, an application to a court may be necessary.

CAN AN ARBITRATOR'S
DECISION BE CHALLENGED?

Either the consumer or the manufacturer may commence a lawsuit to challenge an arbitrator's award within 90 days of receipt of the award. However, the grounds for such challenges are limited by law. Generally, the courts will uphold an arbitrator's award if it is supported by evidence and is grounded in reason. Reasonable attorneys fees may be awarded by the court to a consumer who is successful in challenging or defending an arbitration award.

WHAT ROLE WILL THE ATTORNEY GENERAL'S
OFFICE OR THE AAA PLAY
IF A MANUFACTURER CHALLENGES
AN AWARD IN COURT?

Neither the Attorney General's Office nor the AAA is authorized to represent an individual consumer in such a challenge; this is the responsibility of the consumer's own attorney. In some cases, where the manufacturer raises constitutional issues or questions of general application regarding the lemon law, the Attorney General's Office may seek to intervene in the case to present its position to the court. The AAA's role is administrative; its job is finished when the arbitrator's award is sent to the parties.

CAN CONSUMERS APPLY
FOR ANOTHER HEARING UNDER
THE NEW YORK PROGRAM
IF THEY LOST THE FIRST ONE?

A decision under the New York Program is binding on both parties. However, if new facts arise after a hearing was held, the consumer may reapply for a new hearing based on the new facts. For example, if a consumer originally applied to the New York Program based on four unsuccessful repair attempts (Jan. 5, Jan. 25, Feb. 10, Feb. 25) and lost the arbitration, he or she may reapply if there were four additional repair attempts not previously considered (Apr. 10, Apr. 25, May 10, May 25) even if the repair attempts were for the same problem.

DOES THE LEMON LAW LIMIT
ANY OF THE OTHER
LEGAL REMEDIES
ALREADY AVAILABLE TO CONSUMERS?

The Lemon Law adds to the consumer's arsenal of existing legal remedies. These legal remedies can be explained by the consumer's attorney.

CAN A CONSUMER'S RIGHTS
BE WAIVED UNDER
THE LEMON LAW?

Any contract clause which seeks to waive a consumer's rights under the Lemon Law is void.

HOW IS A USED CAR BUYER PROTECTED
WHEN PURCHASING A CAR PREVIOUSLY
RETURNED TO THE MANUFACTURER
UNDER THE LEMON LAW?

A used car buyer must be given a written, conspicuous disclosure statement by the dealer reading:

> IMPORTANT: THIS VEHICLE WAS RETURNED TO THE MANUFACTURER OR DEALER BECAUSE IT DID NOT CONFORM TO ITS WARRANTY AND THE DEFECT OR CONDITION WAS NOT FIXED WITHIN A REASONABLE TIME AS PROVIDED BY NEW YORK LAW.

This disclosure must also be printed on the car's certificate of title by the New York State Department of Motor Vehicles.

WHERE CAN A CONSUMER GET HELP
OR FURTHER INFORMATION
REGARDING THE LEMON LAW?

A consumer may contact any of the offices of Attorney General Robert Abrams listed at the end of this booklet or consult a lawyer.

APPENDIX C

New York State New and Used Vehicle Lemon Law Arbitration Regulations

ARBITRATION PROGRAM REGULATIONS

*Pursuant to General Business Law
Sections 198-a and 198-b*

Title 13 NYCRR Chap. VIII
Part 300

New York New and Used Car Lemon Law Arbitration Program Regulations

Section 300.1 Purpose

(a) These regulations are promulgated pursuant to the "New York Lemon Law", General Business Law ("GBL") section 198-a, as amended by Chapter 799 of the Laws of 1986, and section 198-b, as amended by Chapter 609 of the Laws of 1989. They set forth the procedures for the operation of an alternative arbitration mechanism (the "Programs") as required by GBL §198-a(k) and GBL §198-b(f)(3).

(b) These regulations are designed to promote the independent, speedy, efficient and fair disposition of disputes concerning defective new and used motor vehicles.

Section 300.2 Definitions

(a) Unless otherwise stated, terms used in these regulations are as defined in GBL §198-a or GBL §198-b.

(b) The term "Administrator" shall mean a professional arbitration firm or individual appointed by the Attorney General to administer the Program.

Section 300.3 Appointment of Administrator

(a) The Attorney General shall appoint an Administrator or Administrators to a definite term not to exceed two years. The term shall be renewable.

(b) The following criteria shall be considered in the selection of an Administrator: capability, objectivity, nonaffiliation with a manufacturer's arbitration program, reliability, experience, financial stability, extent of geographic coverage, and fee structure.

(c) The Attorney General shall give appropriate public notice at least 60 days prior to the expiration of an Administrator's term inviting any interested qualified party to apply in writing for the position of Administrator within 30 days from the date of the public notice.

(d) Upon a vacancy occurring prior to the expiration of an Administrator's term, the time periods in subdivision (3) shall not apply and the Attorney General shall take appropriate steps to assure the continued administration of the Program.

Section 300.4 Consumer's Request for Arbitration

(a) The Attorney General shall prescribe and make available "Request for Arbitration" forms for both GBL §198-a and GBL §198-b claims. To apply for arbitration under the Program, a consumer shall obtain, complete and submit the appropriate form to the Attorney General.

(b) Those consumers wishing a hearing on documents only shall so indicate on the form.

(c) For a GBL §198-a claim, the consumer shall indicate on the form his/her choice of remedy (i.e., either refund or comparable replacement vehicle), in the event the arbitrator rules in favor of the consumer. Such choice shall be followed by the arbitrator unless the consumer advises the Administrator in writing of a change in his/her choice of remedy prior to the arbitrator's rendering of a decision.

(d) Upon receipt, the Attorney General shall date-stamp and assign a case number to the form.

(e) The Attorney General shall review the submitted form for completeness and eligibility and shall either accept it or reject it.

(f) If the form is rejected by the Attorney General, the Attorney General shall promptly return the form, notifying the consumer in writing of the reasons for the rejection and, where possible, inviting the consumer to correct the deficiencies.

(g) If the form is accepted by the Attorney General, he shall refer it to the Administrator for processing. The Attorney General shall promptly notify the consumer in writing of the acceptance of the form and of its referral to the Administrator. Such notice shall also advise the consumer to pay the prescribed filing fee directly to the Administrator.

(h) If, after 30 days from the date of the notice of acceptance, the Administrator fails to receive the prescribed filing fee, the Administrator shall promptly advise the consumer in writing that unless such fee is received within 60 days from the date of the first notice, the form will be returned and the case marked closed. After such time, if the consumer wishes to pursue a claim under the Program, (s)he must submit a new form to the Attorney General.

(i) Participation in any informal dispute resolution mechanism that is not binding on the consumer shall not affect the eligibility of a consumer to participate in either Program.

Section 300.5   Filing Date
On the day the Administrator receives the prescribed filing fee, the Administrator shall date stamp the "Request for Arbitration" form. Such date shall be considered the "filing date".

Section 300.6   Assignment of Arbitrator
(a) After the filing date, the Administrator shall assign an arbitrator to hear and decide the case. Notice of assignment shall be mailed to the arbitrator and the parties along with a copy of these regulations and GBL §198-a or GBL §198-b, whichever is applicable.

(b) The arbitrator assigned shall not have any bias, any financial or personal interest in the outcome of the hearing, or any current connection to the sale or manufacture of motor vehicles.

(c) Upon a finding by the Administrator, at any stage of the process, of grounds to disqualify the arbitrator, the Administrator shall dismiss the arbitrator and assign another arbitrator to the case.

(d) If any arbitrator should resign, die, withdraw or be unable to perform the duties of his/her position, the Administrator shall assign another arbitrator to the case and the period to render a decision shall be extended accordingly.

(e) Arbitrators shall undergo training established by the Administrator and the Attorney General. This training shall include procedural techniques, the duties and responsibilities of arbitrators under the Programs, and the substantive provisions of GBL §198-a for those arbitrators hearing GBL §198-a claims, and the substantive provisions of GBL §198-b for those arbitrators hearing GBL §198-b claims.

Section 300.7   Scheduling of Arbitration Hearings
(a) Each manufacturer of cars sold in New York shall notify the Attorney General in writing, within 10 days after the effective date of these regulations, of the name, address and telephone number of the person designated to receive notices under the GBL

§198-a Program. Such information shall be presumed correct unless updated by the manufacturer.

(b) The arbitration shall be conducted as an oral hearing unless the consumer has requested, on the "Request for Arbitration" form, a hearing on documents only and both parties agree to a documents only hearing; provided, however, that the parties may mutually agree in writing to change the mode of hearing. Upon such change, the parties shall notify the Administrator who shall comply with the request and, where necessary, such request shall waive the 40 day limit in which a decision must be rendered.

(c) Within 5 days of the filing date, the Administrator shall send the manufacturer's designee or the dealer, as appropriate, a copy of the consumer's completed form along with a notice that it may respond in writing. Such response shall be sent in triplicate, within 15 days of the filing date, to the Administrator, who shall promptly forward one copy to the consumer.

(d) The consumer may respond in writing to the manufacturer's or dealer's submission within 25 days of the filing date. Such response shall be sent in triplicate to the Administrator, who shall promptly forward a copy to the manufacturer or the dealer.

(e) An oral hearing, where appropriate, shall be scheduled no later than 35 days from the filing date, unless a later date is agreed to by both parties. The Administrator shall notify both parties of the date, time and place of the hearing at least 8 days prior to its scheduled date.

(f) Hearings shall be scheduled to accommodate, where possible, time-of-day needs of the consumer and the manufacturer or the dealer, including evening and weekend hours.

(g) Hearings shall also be scheduled to accommodate geographic needs of the consumer. Regular hearing sites shall be established at locations designated by the Administrator, including in the following areas: Albany, Binghamton, Buffalo, Nassau County, New York City, Plattsburgh, Poughkeepsie, Rochester, Suffolk County, Syracuse, Utica, Watertown, and Westchester. No hearing site established by the Administrator shall be discontinued without the approval of the Attorney General. In addition, where a regular site is more than 100 miles from the consumer's residence, a hearing must be scheduled at the request of the consumer at a location designated by the Administrator within 100 miles of the consumer's residence.

(h) In unusual circumstances, a party may present its case by telephone, provided that adequate advance notice is given to the Administrator and to the other party. In such cases, the arbitrator and both parties shall be included and the party requesting the telephonic hearing shall pay all costs associated therewith.

Section 300.8   Adjournments

Either party may make a request to reschedule the hearing. Except in unusual circumstances, such request shall be made to the Administrator orally or in writing at least two business days prior to the hearing date. Upon a finding of good cause, the arbitrator may reschedule the hearing. In unusual circumstances, the arbitrator may reschedule the hearing at any time prior to its commencement.

Section 300.9   Request for Additional Information or Documents

(a) A party, by application in writing to the Administrator, may request the arbitrator to direct the other party to produce any documents or information. The arbitrator shall, upon receiving such request, or on his or her own initiative, direct the production of documents or information which she or he believes will reasonably assist a party in presenting his or her case or assist the arbitrator in deciding the case. The arbitrator's direction for the production of documents and information shall allow a reasonable time for the gathering and production of such documents and information.

(b) All documents and information forwarded in compliance with the arbitrator's direction shall be legible and received no later than three business days prior to the date of the hearing. Each party shall bear its own photocopying costs.

(c) Upon failure of a party to comply with the arbitrator's direction to produce documents and/or information, the arbitrator may draw a negative inference concerning any issue involving such documents or information.

(d) The term "documents" in this section shall include, but not be limited to, relevant manufacturer's service bulletins, dealer work orders, diagnoses, bills, and all communications relating to the consumer's claim.

(e) At the request of either party or on his or her own initiative, the arbitrator, when she or he believes it appropriate, may subpoena any witnesses to appear or documents to be presented at the hearing.

Section 300.10   Representation by Counsel or Third Party

Any party may be represented by counsel or assisted by any third party.

Section 300.11   Interpreters

Any party wishing an interpreter shall make the necessary arrangements and assume the costs for such service.

Section 300.12   Hearing Procedure

(a) The conduct of the hearing shall afford each party a full an equal opportunity to present his/her case.

(b) The arbitrator shall administer an oath or affirmation to each individual who testifies.

(c) Formal rules of evidence shall not apply; the parties may introduce any relevant evidence.

(d) The arbitrator shall receive in evidence a decision rendered in a previous arbitration which was not binding on the consumer and give it such weight as the arbitrator deems appropriate.

(e) The arbitrator shall receive relevant evidence of witnesses by affidavit, and such affidavits shall be given such weight as the arbitrator deems appropriate.

(f) The arbitrator shall have discretion to examine or ride in the consumer's vehicle. Both parties shall be afforded the opportunity to be present and accompany the arbitrator on any such examination or ride.

(g) The consumer shall first present evidence in support of his/her claim, and the manufacturer or the dealer, as applicable, shall then present its evidence. Each party may question the witnesses called by the other. The arbitrator may question any party or witness at any time during the hearing.

(h) The arbitrator shall maintain decorum at the hearing.

(i) The arbitrator may request additional evidence after the closing the hearing. All such evidence shall be submitted to the Administrator for transmission to the arbitrator and the parties.

Section 300.13 Hearing on Documents Only

If the hearing is on documents only, all documents shall be submitted to the Administrator no later than 30 days from the filing date. The arbitrator shall render a timely decision based on all documents submitted.

Section 300.14 Defaults

(a) Upon the failure of a party to appear at an oral hearing, the arbitrator shall nevertheless conduct the hearing and render a timely decision based on the evidence presented and documents contained in the file.

(b) If neither party appears at the hearing, the arbitrator shall return the case to the Administrator who shall close it and so notify the parties.

(c) In a documents-only hearing, where the manufacturer or the dealer, fails to respond to the claim, the arbitrator shall render a decision based upon the documents contained in the file.

Section 300.15 Withdrawal or Settlement Prior to Decision

(a) A consumer may withdraw his/her request for arbitration at any time prior to decision. If the Administrator is notified by the consumer of his/her request to withdraw the claim within seven business days of the filing date, the Administrator shall refund the filing fee.

(b) If the parties agree to a settlement more than seven business days after the filing date but prior to the issuance of a decision, they shall notify the Administrator in writing of the terms of the settlement. Upon the request of the parties, the arbitrator shall issue a decision reflecting the settlement.

Section 300.16 The Decision

(a) The arbitrator shall render a decision within 40 days of the filing date which shall be in writing on a form prescribed by the Administrator and approved by the Attorney General. The decision shall be dated and signed by the arbitrator.

(b) In his/her decision, the arbitrator shall determine whether the consumer qualifies for relief pursuant to GBL §198-a or GBL §198-b, as appropriate. If the arbitrator finds that the consumer qualifies, (s)he shall award the specific remedies prescribed by the applicable statute.

(c) The decision shall specify the monetary award where applicable. A calculation of the amount, in accordance with GBL §198-a or GBL §198-b, as applicable, shall be included in the decision. The decision shall also award the prescribed filing fee to a successful consumer.

(d) The decision shall, where applicable, require that any action required by the manufacturer or the dealer, be completed within 30 days from the date the Administrator notifies the manufacturer or the dealer, of the decision.

(e) The Administrator shall review the decision for technical completeness and accuracy and advise the arbitrator of any suggested technical corrections, such as computational, typographical or other minor corrections. Such changes shall be made only with the consent of the arbitrator.

(f) After review, the Administrator shall, within 45 days of the filing date, mail a copy of the final decision to both parties, the arbitrator, and the Attorney General. The date of mailing to the parties shall be date-stamped by the Administrator on the decision as the date of issuance.

(g) Failure to mail the decision to the parties within the specified time period or failure to hold the hearing within the prescribed time shall not invalidate the decision.

(h) The arbitrator's decision is binding on both parties and is final, subject only to judicial review pursuant to CPLR, Article 75. The decision shall include a statement to this effect.

Section 300.17   Recordkeeping

(a) The Administrator shall keep all records pertaining to each arbitration for a period of at least two years and shall make the records of a particular arbitration available for inspection upon written request by a party to that arbitration, and shall make records of all arbitrations available to the Attorney General upon written request.

(b) The Administrator shall maintain such records and statistics for both Programs as are required by GBL §198-a(m)(3).

Section 300.18   Miscellaneous Provisions

(a) All communications between the parties and the arbitrator, other than at oral hearings, shall be directed to the Administrator.

(b) If any provision of these regulations or the application of such provision to any persons or circumstances shall be held invalid, the validity of the remainder of these regulations and the applicability of such provision to other persons or circumstances shall not be affected thereby.

OFFICES OF THE ATTORNEY GENERAL

The Capitol
Albany, New York 12224 . . . .   (518) 474-5481

120 Broadway
New York, New York 10271 . . . .   (212) 341-2345

REGIONAL OFFICES

59-61 Court Street, 7th Floor
Binghamton, New York 13901 . . . .   (607) 773-7797

65 Court Street
Buffalo, New York 14202 . . . .   (716) 847-7184

300 Motor Parkway
Hauppauge, New York 11788 . . . .   (516) 231-2400

211 Station Road, 6th Floor
Mineola, New York 11501 . . . .   (516) 248-3300

Adam Clayton Powell Jr.
State Office Building
163 West 125th Street
New York, New York 10027 . . . .   (212) 870-4475

70 Clinton Street
Plattsburgh, New York 12901. . . . .   (518) 563-8012

235 Main Street
Poughkeepsie, New York 12601 . . . .   (914) 485-3900

144 Exchange Boulevard
Rochester, New York 14614 . . . .   (716) 546-7430

615 Erie Boulevard West
Syracuse, New York 13204 . . . .   (315) 426-4800

207 Genesee Street
Utica, New York 13501 . . . .   (315) 793-2225

317 Washington Street
Watertown, New York 13601. . . . .   (315) 785-2444

202 Mamaroneck Avenue, Suite 400
White Plains, New York 10601 . . . .   (914) 997-6230

APPENDIX D

Fifty State Lemon Law Master Matrix

Appendix D:

Fifty State Lemon Law Master Matrix

This section, as referenced in the text, outlines for the reader all of the states which presently have Lemon Laws on their books. I tried to list the key points of information for each state. The reader should keep in mind that the information provided in the matrix is the result of a layman's (my) research and interpretation of the laws. I strongly recommend that the reader seek legal counsel in order to obtain further definition and clarification of the law for their home state. There are many facets of the laws that are not addressed by the matrix or the notes that follow it.

If your state is not listed on the matrix, I suggest that you contact your local state attorney generals office and ask them to advise and assist you further.

NOTES:

The following is a list of important points of information that should prove useful to the reader when he or she is getting familiar with the law in his or her own state.

* To avoid a bias at arbitration the reader should insure that the procedure that they use is controlled by either a state law or agency. It is my opinion that the consumer will not get a fair deal from any arbitration program that is funded and operated by the automobile manufacturers or dealers.

* The definition of "motor vehicle" is important. New Jersey and Connecticut are two states that include motorcycles as part of their definition. Missouri includes farm equipment.

* Check the statute of limitations, New York allows up to 4 years after delivery for the consumer to start an action against the manufacturer.

* In most cases the defect must be one which is substantial and impairs the use, safety, or value of the motor vehicle.

* The allowance for the court to award legal fees to the consumer are sometimes a double edge sword. By this I mean that if the court feels that the consumer initiated the case for the sole purpose of harassment of the manufacturer, the court may decide to make the consumer pay for the manufacturer's legal and court costs. BE CAREFUL !

* Most laws cover refund of the full purchase price, title, transportation, options, and taxes. Some laws allow a refund of finance charges.

* The laws also allow for a reduction of the refund for the amount of mileage that the consumer put on the vehicle. Each law differs in the method of calculation and the point in time that said usage mileage is recorded.

* The manufacturer has the right to use consumer neglect, misuse, abuse, or accidents as part of their defense.

* Some laws call out business days while others stipulate calendar days in the calculation for the total amount of days that the vehicle was out of service.

* Remedies available to the consumer are generally a refund or replacement vehicle.

* Penalties are built into some laws which allow the consumer to collect additional money per day, in the event that the manufacturer does not comply with the arbitration or court decision.

* The last column on the matrix is entitled "Disclosure on Resale." I felt that it was important to include this point in the listing. It indicates which states are required to label the vehicle as a "LEMON" - if determined so after the arbitration or court hearing. This fact must be told to the consumer who buys the vehicle from the manufacturer during resale.

Such a requirement puts more teeth into the law for the consumer in that it induces the manufacturer to settle the issue prior to the arbitration or court hearing. Rapid settlement helps the manufacturer to avoid additional loss. The resale value of the vehicle will no doubt be less for one which is legally deemed and labeled as a "LEMON". Such a label might cause the manufacturer to incur additional costs if he elects to ship and sell the vehicle in a neighboring state that does not have a Lemon Law.

If this requirement is on the books for your state, use it to your advantage.

* Lastly, several columns are either marked yes or left intentionally blank. Where blank, I urge the reader to research the point further and consult with a lawyer.

STATE	TYPE	STATUTE SECTION #	COVERAGE	MIN # OF REPAIRS	LOSS OF VEHICLE	ARBITRATION REQUIRED	LEGAL FEES AWARDED	DISCLOSURE ON RESALE
Alabama	New	8-20A-1	1 Year or 12,000 Miles	3	30 days	Yes	Yes	Yes
Alaska	New	45.45 300-360	Express Warranty or 1 Year	3	30 days	Yes		Yes
Arizona	New	44-1261	Express Warranty or 1 Year	4	30 days	Yes		
California	New	1793.2	1 Year or 12,000 miles	4	30 days	Yes	Yes	Yes
Colorado	New	42-12-101	Express Warranty or 1 Year	4	30 days	Yes		
Connecticut **	New	42-179 42-181	2 Years or 18,000 Miles	4	30 days	Yes	Yes	Yes
Delaware	New	5001 - 5009	Express Warranty or 1 Year	4	30 days	Yes	Yes	Yes
District of Columbia	New	20-1301 40-1301	2 Years or 18,000 miles	4	30 days	Yes		Yes
Florida	New	681.104	1 Year or 12,000 Miles	3	30 days	Yes	Yes	
Georgia	New	10-1-780	1 Year or 12,000 miles	3	30 days	Yes		Yes

STATE	TYPE	STATUTE SECTION #	COVERAGE	MIN # OF REPAIRS	LOSS OF VEHICLE	ARBITRATION REQUIRED	LEGAL FEES AWARDED	DISCLOSURE ON RESALE
Hawaii	New	490:2-313.1	Express Warranty	3	30 days	Yes		
Idaho	New	48-901	1 Year or 12,000 miles	4	30 days	Yes		
Illinois	New	Rev. Stat. 1905	1 Year or 12,000 Miles	4	30 days	Yes		
Indiana	New	24-5-13	18 Months or 18,000 miles	4	30 days	Yes	Yes	Yes
Iowa	New	Code 322 E.1	Express Warranty or 1 Year	4	30 days	Yes		
Kansas	New	50-645	Express Warranty or 1 Year	4	30 days	Yes		
Kentucky	New	357.840 through 357.846	1 Year or 12,000 Miles	4	30 days	Yes	Yes	
Louisiana	New	51.1941 through 51.1948	Express Warranty or 1 Year	4	30 days	Yes	Yes	
Maine	New	title 10 1161	2 Years or 18,000 miles	3	15 days	Yes	Yes	Yes
Maryland	New	14-1501 14-1501	15,000 miles or 15 months	4	30 days		Yes	Yes
Massachusetts**	New	7N 1/2	1 Year or 15,000 Miles	3	15 days	Yes	Yes	Yes
Michigan	New	257.1401	Express Warranty or 1 year	4	30 days	Yes		

STATE	TYPE	STATUTE SECTION #	COVERAGE	MIN # OF REPAIRS	LOSS OF VEHICLE	ARBITRATION REQUIRED	LEGAL FEES AWARDED	DISCLOSURE ON RESALE
Minnesota **	New	325F.665	Express Warranty or 2 years	4	30 days	Yes		Yes
Mississippi	New	63-17-151	Express Warranty or 1 Year	3	15 days	Yes		Yes
Missouri	New	407.560 through 407.592	Express Warranty or 1 Year	4	30 days	Yes	Yes	
Montana	New	61-4-501	2 Years or 18,000 miles	4	30 days	Yes		Yes
Nebraska	New	60-2701	Express Warranty or 1 year	4	40 days	Yes	Yes	
Nevada	New	598.751	Express Warranty or 1 Year	4	30 days	Yes		
New Hampshire	New	357D	Express Warranty or 1 Year	4	30 days	Yes		
New Jersey	New	56:12-29	2 Years or 18,000 Miles	3	20 days		Yes	
New Mexico	New	57-16A-L	Express Warranty or 1 Year	4	30 days	Yes		Yes
New York	New	198a	2 Years or 18,000 Miles	4	30 days	Yes	Yes	Yes

STATE	TYPE	STATUTE SECTION #	COVERAGE	MIN # OF REPAIRS	LOSS OF VEHICLE	ARBITRATION REQUIRED	LEGAL FEES AWARDED	DISCLOSURE ON RESALE
New York	Used	198b	60 Days or 3,000 Miles	3	15 Days	Yes	Yes	
North Carolina	New	20-351	Express Warranty or 1 year	4	20 days	Yes	Yes	
North Dakota	New	51-07-16	Express Warranty or 1 year	3	30 days	Yes	Yes	Yes
Ohio	New	1345.71	1 Year or 18,000 miles	3	30 days	Yes	Yes	Yes
Oklahoma	New	tit. 15 901	Express Warranty or 1 year	4	45 days	Yes		
Oregon	New	646.315	1 Year or 12,000 miles	4	30 days	Yes	Yes	
Pennsylvania	New	1951	1 Year or 12,000 miles	3	30 days	Yes	Yes	Yes
Rhode Island **	New	31-5.2-1	1 Year or 15,000 miles	4	30 days	Yes	Yes	Yes
South Carolina	New	56-28-10	1 Year or 12,000 miles	3	30 days	Yes	Yes	Yes
Tennessee	New	55-24-201	Express Warranty or 1 Year	4	30 days	Yes	Yes	
Texas	New	art. 4413	Express Warranty or 1 Year	4	30 days	Yes		

STATE	TYPE	STATUTE SECTION #	COVERAGE	MIN # OF REPAIRS	LOSS OF VEHICLE	ARBITRATION REQUIRED	LEGAL FEES AWARDED	DISCLOSURE ON RESALE
Utah	New	13-20-1	Express Warranty or 1 Year	4	30 days	Yes		
Vermont	New	tit. 9 4170	Express Warranty	3	30 days	Yes		Yes
Virginia	New	59.1-207.11	18 Months	3	30 days	Yes		
Washington	New	19.118	2 Years or 24,000 miles	4	30 days	Yes		Yes
West Virginia	New	46A - 6A-1	Express Warranty or 1 Year	3	30 days	Yes	Yes	Yes
Wisconsin	New	218.015	Express Warranty or 1 Year	4	30 days	Yes	Yes	Yes
Wyoming	New	40-17-101	1 Year	3	30 days	Yes	Yes	Yes

** These States have some form of Used Vehicle Lemon Law. The reader should contact their local State Attorney General Office or law library to obtain additional information on these laws.

Law for the Layperson
LEGAL ALMANACS
Second Series

HOMESELLERS' STRATEGIES IN A SOFT MARKET.
Jeremy D. Smith. ISBN: 0-379-111802.

REGULATING THE ENVIRONMENT: AN OVERVIEW OF FEDERAL ENVIRONMENTAL LAWS. Neil Stoloff. ISBN: 0-379-11173X.

LAW OF RAPE. Irving J. Sloan. ISBN: 0-379-111713.

LEGAL RIGHTS AND REMEDIES FOR THE ELDERLY.
Irving J. Sloan. ISBN: 0-379-111780.

LEMONAID. Andrew Faglio. ISBN: 0-379-111810.

WILLS & TRUSTS, 6th Edition. Orig. by Parnell Callahan. Revised & Edited, Oceana Editorial Staff. ISBN: 111705.

LAW OF MALPRACTICE. Irving J. Sloan. ISBN: 0-379-111748.

EVERYDAY LEGAL FORMS. Irving J. Sloan. ISBN: 0-379-111772.

Oceana's LEGAL ALMANACS

SURROGATE PARENTING AND THE LAW OF ADOPTION.
Irving J. Sloan. ISBN: 0-379-111691.

CIVIL LIBERTY AND CIVIL RIGHTS. 7th Edition. E.S. Newman & Dan Moretti.
ISBN: 0-379-111608.

JUVENILE OFFENDERS & THE JUVENILE JUSTICE SYSTEM. 2nd Edition.
Sol Rubin. ISBN: 0-379-111500.

FORENSIC PSYCHIATRY & LEGAL PROTECTION OF THE INSANE. 2nd Edition.
Stanley Pearlstein. ISBN: 0-379-111527.

THE CRIME AND PUNISHMENT PRIMER. 3rd Edition. Bertha White.
ISBN: 0-379-111519.

REGULATING LAND USE: THE LAW OF ZONING. Irving J. Sloan. ISBN: 0-379-111659.

HOMOSEXUAL CONDUCT AND THE LAW: THE LEGAL STANDING OF GAYS AND LESBIANS.
Irving J. Sloan. ISBN: 0-379-111616.

PUBLIC INTEREST LAW: WHERE LAW MEETS SOCIAL ACTION. R. Baum.
ISBN: 0-379-111624.

THE LAWS GOVERNING ABORTION, CONTRACEPTION & STERILIZATION. Irving J. Sloan.
ISBN: 0-379-111632.

THE HOME MORTGAGE LAW PRIMER. Irving J. Sloan. ISBN: 0-379-111640.

AIDS LAW: IMPLICATIONS FOR THE INDIVIDUAL AND SOCIETY. Irving J. Sloan.
ISBN: 0-379-111667.